Project Management and Human Resources

How to Use Agile, Scrum, Lean Six Sigma, Kanban and Kaizen for Managing Projects Along with a Guide on Human Resource Management

© Copyright 2021

The content contained within this book may not be reproduced, duplicated, or transmitted without direct written permission from the author or the publisher.

Under no circumstances will any blame or legal responsibility be held against the publisher or author for any damages, reparation, or monetary loss due to the information contained within this book, either directly or indirectly.

Legal Notice:

This book is copyright protected. It is only for personal use. You cannot amend, distribute, sell, use, quote, or paraphrase any part of the contents within this book without the consent of the author or publisher.

Disclaimer Notice:

Please note the information contained within this document is for educational and entertainment purposes only. All effort has been executed to present accurate, up to date, reliable, complete information. No warranties of any kind are declared or implied. Readers acknowledge that the author is not engaging in the rendering of legal, financial, medical, or professional advice. The content within this book has been derived from various sources. Please consult a licensed professional before attempting any techniques outlined in this book.

By reading this document, the reader agrees that under no circumstances is the author responsible for any losses, direct or indirect, that are incurred as a result of the use of the information contained within this document, including, but not limited to, errors, omissions, or inaccuracies.

Contents

PART 1: PROJECT MANAGEMENT 1
INTRODUCTION 2
CHAPTER 1 – PROJECT MANAGEMENT: 5
BEFORE YOU START 5
    What is Project Management? 5
    The Core Components of Project Management 7
    Top Project Management Methodologies 10
    Your Role as Project Manager 14
CHAPTER 2 – AGILE AND SCRUM 16
    What is Agile Project Management? 16
    The Benefits of Agile 23
    Scrum: All You Need to Know 29
    Agile Applied – Eight Best Practices 39
    Is Your Team Agile? 42
    Common Agile Fails and Solutions 44
CHAPTER 3 – LEAN SIX SIGMA 48
    What is Lean Six Sigma? 48
    Waste: Explanation and Elimination Tips 53
    Tools and concepts for Lean Six Sigma 59
    Value Stream Mapping Hacks You Should Know 64
    DMAIC vs. DMADV 71
    How to Apply Lean Analytics 75

Mastering Lean Six Sigma Roles 78

Where to use Lean Six Sigma 79

CHAPTER 4 – KANBAN AND KAIZEN 81

Kanban and Kaizen Defined and Compared 81

Ways to Apply Kanban 85

Implementing Kaizen in Your Company 87

Personal Kaizen 92

Kanban With or Without Kaizen? 93

CONCLUSION 95

RESOURCES 97

PART 2: HUMAN RESOURCE MANAGEMENT 101

INTRODUCTION 102

CHAPTER 1: WHAT IS HUMAN RESOURCE MANAGEMENT (HRM)? 104

WHAT IS HRM? 105

HISTORICAL DEVELOPMENT OF HRM 107

WHY HUMAN RESOURCE MANAGEMENT? 110

FUNCTIONS OF HUMAN RESOURCES MANAGEMENT 113

CHAPTER 2: BASIC THEORIES AND APPROACHES OF HRM 115

THE HUMAN RELATIONS THEORY OF MANAGEMENT 116

HUMAN RELATIONS MANAGEMENT THEORIES 120

HOW MASLOW'S THEORY FITS WITH HUMAN RELATIONS IN MANAGEMENT 122

ORGANIZATION LIFE CYCLE THEORY 124

FIVE STAGES OF THE ORGANIZATION'S LIFE CYCLE 124

THE "SOFT" AND "HARD" APPROACHES TO HUMAN RESOURCE MANAGEMENT 127

CHAPTER 3: THE HR MANAGER AND OTHER KEY ROLES 129

ROLES OF A HUMAN RESOURCE MANAGER 130

HOW TO MONITOR AND EVALUATE YOUR PROGRESS 133

CHAPTER 4: ONBOARDING AND RECRUITING TACTICS 140

Why Onboarding and Recruitment Matters 141
Recruitment Planning 142
Talent Sourcing 144
Screening of Applicants 147
Onboarding 150
Onboarding Tips 152
21st Century Recruitment Tips 152

CHAPTER 5: PERFORMANCE MANAGEMENT STRATEGIES 154
What is Performance Management? 155
Why is Performance Management Important? 155
Importance of Performance Management 156
Strategies in Performance Management 158
Real-World Business Examples of Performance Management 162
Performance Management Best Practices in HRM 163
Performance Management Tools 163

CHAPTER 6: PAYROLL, COMPENSATION, AND BENEFITS 165
What is Payroll? 165
Payroll Cycle 166
Human Resource Management and Payroll Activities 166
Pros and Cons of Outsourcing Payroll Services 167
Compensation 168
Internal Alignment 170
External Competitiveness 171
Compensation Management 172
Employee Benefits 173
Difference Between Payroll and Compensation 174

CHAPTER 7: MAINTAINING POSITIVE EMPLOYEE RELATIONS (ER) 175
What are Employee Relations? 175
How to Build Strong Employee Relationships 177
The Power of Positive Employee Relations 179

WHAT ARE EMPLOYEE RELATIONS PROCESSES? 182

EMPLOYEE RELATIONS POLICIES.. 183

EMPLOYEE RELATIONS BEST PRACTICES 184

CHAPTER 8: LEGAL CONSIDERATIONS 188

DISCRIMINATION CHARGES 189

LEGAL CONSIDERATIONS TIPS AND WARNINGS 195

CHAPTER 9: FIVE COMMON HRM MISTAKES TO AVOID............. 198

CHAPTER 10: HRM TECHNOLOGY AND TRENDS............................ 209

THE IMPACT OF TECHNOLOGICAL INNOVATION IN HUMAN RESOURCE
MANAGEMENT 210

HUMAN RESOURCE MANAGEMENT SOFTWARE... 211

TOP HUMAN RESOURCE MANAGEMENT SOFTWARE................................. 214

HRM TRENDS OF 2020 215

RETURN OF INVESTMENT OF HR CHATBOT 219

APPENDIX: HUMAN RESOURCES GLOSSARY 222

REFERENCES 225

Part 1: Project Management

An Essential Guide for Beginners Who Want to Understand Agile, Scrum, Lean Six Sigma, Kanban and Kaizen When Applied to Managing Projects

Introduction

Projects are a way of launching your organization into the future. Whether it is the US Government building a new generation of fighter planes, a major bank launching an asset finance division, a software company developing new functionality, or a corporate building its new headquarters, you only have to read the papers and see a whole load of projects being started, progressed, and completed… only to end up as failures.

According to KPMG's PMI Pulse of the Profession report,

- 48% of projects are not finished in time;
- 43% spend more than the expected budget; and
- 31% don't meet the original goals of the project.

This adds up to more than 100%, which is pretty startling. (Of course, the answer is that some projects are late *and* over budget; some are over budget *and* fail to meet the objectives… And some are late, over budget, *and* failures, which makes them a complete waste of money, time, and resources.)

Some projects were always bound to fail. However, that is just a tiny minority. (Perhaps nothing could have saved New Coke.) Most projects fail at least partly because of poor project management. If the project manager does not keep the team focused, doesn't keep control of progress, and doesn't keep checking that the project is meeting its objectives, projects easily drift. It is like letting a boat sail on without keeping a hand on the tiller—sooner or later, it will drift off course.

That makes project management one of the key management disciplines for the current times. But if you have come across project management in your daily work, you will know that it can be full of buzz words, methodologies, reporting schemas, charts—an impenetrable forest of jargon.

This book aims to demystify project management and show you two different approaches that have a big following: Agile/Scrum, a very free form methodology that is good for services and software, and Lean Six Sigma, which is more data-driven and particularly useful for high-volume businesses from call centers to manufacturing.

Kanban and Kaizen, Japanese approaches to improving quality, will also be discussed. While these are not project management methodologies as such, they are beneficial ways to improve a project's productivity. They can also really get project team members fired up—which is another part of the project manager's job.

The aim here is not to get you through Lean Six Sigma certification—you will have to take a course for that—or enable you to take on your own Scrum project on Monday morning. Most professional project managers will tell you it took them several years and several projects before they really got rolling. However, you will be given the basics so that you are not only familiar with the different methodologies, but have a feel for which one suits your personal style and the organization you work for.

Project management jargon will further be clarified, along with how the processes work. If you have to contribute to someone else's project, you will have a better feel for how things should work; if you have a project of your own to run, you'll have a gentler learning curve.

And if you are working in a start-up, or you have a small family business, then you won't need certification or expensive paperwork to get started managing your projects. This book will give you the gist of how to run a project, keep your team motivated, and achieve your objectives.

Remember: Objectives are what project management is all about. Be clear about the objectives first and foremost—and keep referring back to them to avoid "scope creep"—, and you won't go too far wrong. But if you forget your objectives and get mired in the project charts and workflow, it will be easy to miss the target by a long way.

Chapter 1 – Project Management: Before You Start

What is Project Management?

Project management can be seen as simply "Getting a project done", and in a nutshell, that is it.

However, more technically, you could call it the application of different processes to achieve your specific project objectives. You are applying knowledge, skills, and experience to the task—your own if you're managing the project and the capabilities of the team members who may have their own specialist skills to contribute.

Project management is focused on achieving the objectives within agreed parameters (on time, on budget) and according to project acceptance criteria (such as quality and specification).

A simple instance might be the project of building a house. The house is your final deliverable. You have a budget and a timescale as constraints—it has to be ready by a certain date, and your materials and labor must not cost more than the budget. Your client will also have given you specifications, such as the quality of finish and perhaps the energy rating, as well as basics, such as the number of bedrooms and bathrooms.

Project management has to deliver all of this—not just some of it, *all* of it.

- The house is great, but you're over budget – fail.
- You're on budget, and the house is exactly what the client wanted, but he's been living in an RV for two months waiting for you to finish – fail.
- On time, under budget, but the plastering and painting look rather amateurish, and one of the bathrooms hasn't been plumbed in – fail.
- On time, under budget, to spec. But you didn't get the paperwork done, and the building inspector won't sign it off – fail.

(Oh yes, project management is also about the paper trail, and getting things documented properly.)

If you were a house builder, you might think that your job is "building". However, if you are a project manager running a building site, you know your job is not "building" but "managing a build", and that those are two different things. Project management is not about plastering or wiring or laying bricks; it is about managing the materials, the personnel, and your finances to ensure the house is ready on time and to budget.

Every commercial builder will tell you that good craftspeople can be appalling project managers. Good finance people can also be terrible project managers—the skills you need to put together a great finance package are not the same as those you will need to run a building project!

But project management is not the same as ordinary management. If you run a factory, for instance, you will be running "business as usual", day after day. The factory operates continuously, and you expect to carry on running it for the foreseeable future. Project management, on the other hand, has a finite timescale. When the project is completed, you are done. Often, time is of the essence—for instance, getting a new product out before your competitors, or finishing a new building so your client can move in on a certain date. The date might be a regulatory requirement (like new requirements on managing client data within a software system), a client requirement (as in the case of the house), or it might reflect the market (ready for the holiday season).

If you choose a career as a "regular" manager, you will probably work most of the time in the same division and functional area—human resources, operations, marketing, or finance, for instance. You'll probably live within one of the "silos" of the business. As a project manager, on the other hand, you may never work on the same area twice; every project will be different. Within a large organization, you'll probably end up working across the functional divide, and you may have to manage teams with members seconded from different areas of the business or different functions. You may even manage external team members, such as consultants and customer or supplier staff.

Many people love project management precisely because of the challenge it represents. You are always under time pressure, and the job is always throwing you new challenges. If this is the kind of environment in which you thrive—if you just can't imagine yourself doing the same thing all day, every day—, then project management is for you.

The Core Components of Project Management

Below is a break down of a typical project that looks at its different core components, beginning with the creation of the project, which is often before the project manager comes on board. However, if you are asked to run a project, you will want to look at those basic requirements and resources before you take the job—make sure they are realistic; otherwise, you'll be taking a poisoned chalice.

First, define your project. Why is this project necessary? It might be "to save money and improve profit margins" or "to meet regulatory approval requirements", or "to counter our competitor's new product with a better one". If you don't know *why* you want to carry out the project, it's not a good one. (For instance, given the example of the house, does the client want to live in it or rent it out? No one orders a house just because they fancy spending money, and depending on the answer, the specifications and timescales might be different.)

Capture the project requirements. These will include the delivery date, budget, and specifications. If they are vague or unrealistic, you will need to do some negotiating and perhaps remind your client or manager of the **iron triangle**—which is discussed later.

Capture the project resources. What do you have to work with? For instance, what personnel are you being given to carry out the work? What data do you have available (for instance, data on the market segment you are addressing or on the current performance of the processes you're aiming to improve)? Are particular materials being provided?

At this point, you should prepare the business case. Quite simply, given the resources being consumed, is the project going to be worthwhile?

Getting funding or sponsorship is the next step. That might be getting funding from a bank, but it's more likely to be securing the support of a senior manager within a large business.

Now the project manager's work begins properly. First, you'll need to develop a project plan that needs to break the project down into several steps—for instance, for the example of a house build, acquisition of the land, design, site preparation, masonry, roofing, interior works, finishing, and decoration. You'll want to think about dependencies; for instance, you can't put the roof on until the walls are ready (though you *could* start on the frames for the roof); you can't do the drywalling till the wiring is finished.

And next, you implement the plan.

Then, you'll need to monitor progress against the plan, and as part of developing the plan, you should have created processes for measuring and evaluating your progress. (As you'll see, some PM methodologies will help you a great deal with this.) If things go wrong, go back to the plan, and see what you can change to keep on track—or go back to the client and ask them what their preferred course of action is.

The project manager's job isn't just about accounting, planning, and monitoring; you'll also need to provide leadership. You're the person on the team with the vision of the whole project and how it fits your client's or sponsor's requirements. You have to communicate that vision to your team and keep them motivated.

You may need to manage external service or product providers.

You need to keep your customer/sponsor informed. You might also be responsible for dealing with other stakeholders, such as employees in areas of the business that will be affected by your project, or the neighbors in the case of the building site example.

And finally, you'll need to deliver the project, with any training, documentation, or implementation plans that are required.

Project management is an iterative process. For instance, if when developing the project plan, you find there is a resource missing, or a dependency that means the project needs more time than expected, you will need to go back and discuss that with the client.

If you find there is a difficulty—a supplier delivers materials late, or someone finds a software dependency that hadn't been identified and will require time for integration—then again, you'll need to go back and check, and perhaps change, the plan.

And this is where the **iron triangle** needs to be explained. Every project has three requirements or constraints:

1. budget
2. speed
3. specification

As an old builder once said, "You can have it fast and good, or good and cheap, or cheap and fast. But you can't have it fast *and* cheap *and* good." You can move two points of the triangle, but you can't move all three. And if you are going to become a good project manager, you have to acquire a sixth sense for which one of those three points is the one your client will be *really* unhappy to see moved.

Top Project Management Methodologies

PM, like all areas of management, has developed its own methodologies and tools. This book will tell you about the most recent and most well-known methodologies and show you how they work. Here is a summary of the basics of each one.

Agile was created as a tool for managing software development projects in 2001. Most traditional PM processes were designed for manufacturing or high-volume service companies and were not particularly useful for software. Agile is particularly good for incremental projects, such as building a system piece by piece or creating extra modules for existing software.

Agile is iterative rather than linear, like traditional PM methods. In Agile, you design the program, test it, make changes and improvements, re-test. It is also collaborative, working across functional teams. That is hugely important when you are designing in-house software that other parts of the business will use.

Plus, Agile is designed for the sort of environment where you have highly skilled people working on the project—a software house, a design studio, or a finance business, for instance. It prioritizes individuals and their interactions, rather than processes and tools. Rather than seeing the relationship with the customer as a contract, Agile envisions it as a collaboration.

Agile is pragmatic. It aims to deliver working software, rather than documentation, and it makes it easy to respond to change while following the project plan. Changing requirements can be accommodated throughout the process because of its iterative nature.

Lean Six Sigma

Six Sigma is a project management methodology that was developed at Motorola in the 1980s. It gets its name from the "six sigma" statistic, a measurement of variance from the mean—in other words; it focuses on improving quality by ensuring the outcomes of your processes do not vary. Suppose you are in a call center, and you want most people to have their calls answered in ten seconds, but if that average conceals a huge difference between some people who have the phone picked up right away, and some who wait half an hour, you're not doing all that well. Six Sigma concentrates on reducing that variance.

So, Six Sigma methodology looks at reducing errors by identifying and removing what is not working. It is a methodology that's highly suited for large corporates because it's data-driven—and it's highly relevant for companies focusing on low-cost production.

Lean Six Sigma forked from the base methodology in 2001 and expanded its remit from manufacturing into finance, healthcare, and logistics. Like its "parent" methodology, it focuses on reducing eight kinds of waste, summed up in the acronym DOWNTIME: defects, overproduction, waiting, non-utilized talent, transport, inventory, motion, and extra processing—these are looked at in more detail later.

Kanban

Kanban is not a methodology so much as a project management tool, but it is a very useful one, often used within both Agile and Six Sigma projects.

Kanban emerged from Japanese shop floor management. Sticky notes were applied to a wall chart that showed three columns—things to be done, work in progress, and completed work. Imagine, in a factory, the product backlog, work actually being done, and stocks of completed work—very simply managed by moving the sticky notes from one column to the next. Now, Kanban software is available that not only lets you "post" your "sticky notes" in the right column, but it can also tell you how quickly you are completing tasks and how long it should take to complete the backlog.

Visualization is critical in the way people think about things, and by giving a clear picture of the work-flow process, kanban can really help a project. It is a highly democratic tool, enabling any member of the team to pick a task, but it's also good at prioritizing and ensuring tasks are completed.

As well as visualizing, kanban helps to focus the team by limiting the amount of work in progress—there may be a rule of "only three tasks to be in progress at any time". That can stop team members going off at a tangent and wasting time on less important tasks.

Kaizen

Kaizen often goes along with kanban. Kaizen is the Japanese word for "improvement", and the term is applied to a management philosophy based on continuous improvement. It is particularly useful in companies with highly standardized systems and processes.

Kaizen is about flow and process. Often, it can generate small improvements that can be made within one or two days. Kaizen delivers responsibility to every member of the organization; if a shop floor worker comes up with an idea for improvement, it is just as valid as the CEO's big idea. That means that though Kaizen goes along with standardization, the way it brings about those standards is very different from the Taylorian "command and control" standardization-from-the-top with which many people are familiar.

Kaizen applied to "business as usual" is one of the factors that made the Japanese manufacturer industry great. However, it can also be used as part of project management, particularly within an iterative process. As your project team learns from experience, that learning can be built into the project—whether that is by incorporating new code into the software you are writing or improving the project's processes.

Scrum

Scrum is a subset of Agile project management that focuses on using short time-boxed bursts of activity, called Sprints. It has five values: commitment, courage, focus, openness, and respect. Like Agile, it is an iterative process and one which promotes collaboration.

A Sprint might aim to deliver a new app, for instance, in two weeks, as part of an overall Scrum project updating a company's marketing software. Within the Sprint, the daily Scrum is a fifteen-minute meeting, discussing the previous day's achievements, expectations for the day's work, and any blocks to progress (for instance, having to wait for an external company to provide input). Short stand-up meetings, quick time frames, and intense focus can make Scrum a very productive project management process.

It also builds learning into the project, with Sprint reviews and retrospective meetings focused on learning from the last Sprint and carrying any learning points back into the main project.

Sprint is demanding—there is nowhere to hide. But for smaller teams who are well motivated and need flexibility, it is a really great project management methodology. Some tech staff won't use anything else.

Your Role as Project Manager

Project Managers are all different. Some have their Gantt charts at their fingertips. Some are inspirational leaders. Some are good at handling an organization's internal politics. Others are terrific at working with external consultants and contractors.

However, while your mix of skills and the way you use them will be different from anyone else's—no two project managers are the same—, you need certain basic skills and aptitudes.

- *Love of the new.* Managing change is a crucial part of project management, so you need to enjoy change yourself. Otherwise, how can you encourage other people to change?
- *Flexibility.* There's no right or wrong way to project manage; there are different tools, methods, people, and cultures. As a project manager, you'll need to be flexible—to be able to suit your tools and style to the circumstances.
- *Analytic smarts.* You will need to be able to work out complex dependencies and consider how each small detail affects the project overall. You'll certainly need to manage budgets and planning.
- *Strategic vision.* While as a project manager, you'll spend much of your time chasing detail, you need to see the overall strategy of the project. You also need to communicate that to your team so they can see where their effort fits into the overall picture.
- *People skills.* You'll need slightly different skills from direct line management. You may need to recruit your staff; you need to be able to motivate them. Remember: These may be people whose more important full-time job is elsewhere, so you need to find a reason people should care about your project.

- *Task orientation.* If you're the kind of person who's focused on processes rather than outcomes, you may not be best suited to project management. While processes are important, project managers have to focus on delivering the project requirement—that's the number one job!
- Great project managers will tell you there's a *sixth sense* that helps them detect problems when they're talking to customers, suppliers, and team members. The signs of unease may be very subtle—someone not meeting your eyes, or being unhappy about giving you a commitment to a definite date—but you need to pick them up.
- You'll also need to be a *good negotiator.* This isn't about getting a better price or more time; it's about balancing the different needs of the projects, its team members, and stakeholders.

Good project managers can have well-paid and fascinating careers. You might progress from project manager to program manager, managing more than one project at a time. It is not an easy career; you will need to understand a lot more than just project management. One IT project manager said, "I have to understand accounting as well as the CFO, marketing as well as the marketing department do, and programming nearly as well as my best programmer. And then I have to get the project delivered." *That* is the bit they pay her for!

However, it is a great career if you like variety. It's a great career if you like a challenge. And even if you never become a full-time project manager, understanding how to define and run a project will give you a head start in any area of business.

Chapter 2 – Agile and Scrum

What is Agile Project Management?

If you were brought up with traditional project management tools, Agile could make you feel rather vulnerable. It is basically a set of values and themes rather than a PM tool. It helps teams progress quickly, and it's a PM management process that is designed to enable teams to provide quick responses to feedback.

Since the project is continuously being reassessed, Agile is ideal for the kind of project where the project requirements might change throughout the life of the project. Arguably, earlier styles of project management, in which the project definition is set for once and for all at inception, were useful in a relatively static world. But in a more turbulent and dynamic environment, Agile is better able to keep up with events. If you were developing a business software project when cloud computing came on the horizon, following old-style project management techniques, you would have ended up delivering an already obsolete project to time and budget. On the other hand, Agile would have let you continue to upgrade and improve the product, so it remained relevant to the new environment of cloud computing and distributed software.

A more theoretical way of putting this would be to say that Agile is heuristic, recursive where traditional waterfall projects are linear, algorithmic, and programmed.

Agile divides the project into several separate iterations that have two big benefits:

- The project objective is delivered incrementally, not all at once. So, for instance, one module of a software requirement might be delivered and already in use before the whole project remit has been met.

- The project is continuously being reassessed, using what has been learned or delivered in previous iterations to refine the project specification and processes. All project teams learn on the job—but Agile puts that learning into use.

Obviously, with the example of the project "build a house", Agile does not have huge advantages. However, if you think instead about building a multi-house, multi-phase development, Agile might help refine the project in various ways.

- In the first phase, potential buyers all headed for the smaller homes. That gives you a chance to change the mix of homes being delivered in the next phase, to meet market demand.

- Halfway through your first phase, one of your suppliers started offering modular bathrooms. If you change the spec and use these instead of plumbing in from scratch, you can save 20% on bathroom costs.

- You've managed to compress build times by 5%. You can now refine your target dates for the remaining phrases of the project accordingly.

(Actually, you probably wouldn't use Agile on a construction project. But it's an example everyone can understand; if you're not a geek, using software examples wouldn't give you much idea of what's going on in the project.)

Traditional projects are run based on a contract with the customer. The project is set up via a contract negotiation. Instead, Agile prefers to see the customer as a collaborator. Discussing changes to the contract, then, is not like negotiating variances, which all have a cost; it is more about refining the customer's needs and getting their input and feedback throughout the project.

That means customers are more involved. In a traditional project, they are really only involved upfront, and then when the project is delivered, in signing it off. They get progress reports, but if things go according to plan, they don't need to do anything. In Agile, on the other hand, they are continuously talking to the project manager about the project. They will look at what has been delivered, for instance, because there is always one task being completed, such as finished software being released. That means an Agile project manager's job will include much customer liaison compared to the traditional project manager's role.

Twelve principles of Agile software development

You can get a good feeling for how Agile works by considering the twelve principles of agile software development. Even if you don't go the whole Agile route, they are not bad principles to apply in any project, particularly in software design projects:

1 **Continuity.** Deliver customer satisfaction by delivering the project continuously. So, for instance, a software project will deliver working software continuously, not keeping everything for the end.

2 **Changing requirements**. Always be willing to accept a change in requirements at any stage of the project. The project is a living thing—not a dead project plan.

3 **Short timescales.** Deliver software that works within a shorter timescale. Focus on reducing the time taken to deliver the objectives of the project.

4 **Daily collaboration.** Team members must work together daily. Agile isn't the kind of project where some team members only do a few hours a week. It's intense, and it demands full-time collaboration.

5 **Face to face.** Face-to-face conversations are the best way to transfer knowledge and get things done. Don't rely on email or phone.

6 **Motivate and empower.** Motivate people to build a project by creating an environment of appreciation, trust, and empowerment. This is really key to Agile—if you want to micro-manage people, Agile is not for you!

7 **Working software.** Working software is the key measure of progress. (Applying Agile outside the software field, you'll want to look at other deliverable outcomes, of course—but the key is that they *work* and are complete, that they have value, and are delivered throughout the life of the project.)

8 **Sustainable development.** An Agile team should be able to keep producing at a steady pace. Agile isn't a big effort and then a burn-out process—it's like running a marathon.

9 **Quality.** Continuous attention to excellence and quality in technical development and design boosts agility. Don't cut corners, and don't let standards slip.

10 **Keep it simple.** Simplicity is a vital part of effective agile management.

11 **The self-organizing team.** Self-organized teams produce the best architecture, requirements, and design. Team members should be able to set their work pace, allocate work around the team, and keep track of how they are doing—the project manager doesn't need to micro-manage them.

12 **Reflection.** Teams should reflect through inspection and adaption to be more effective. Continuously assessing what has been done so far, and learning from that experience, makes Agile teams able to improve not just their software but their working process and capabilities.

That is quite a big chunk of principles, so below it's been broken down into some central concepts; continuity/iteration, short timescales, learning, empowerment, and openness:

- *Continuity and iteration* – keep on delivering, not all-at-once but continuously; going back to the project plan and refining it continually; and keeping going at a steady pace, not throwing your project team at the wall to meet a deadline. "Repeat and review" is a common theme.

- *Short timescales* – even in a long-term project, keep the immediate timescales short. It's better to deliver one breakfast every morning rather than 365 breakfasts on day 364, even if that does technically "bring in" your project one day before it's due!

- *Learning* – Agile is an adaptive system. The team and the project manager should always be learning and applying that learning to improve the project deliverables and the process. If you learn that a particular technique makes life easier, write it into the project spec!

- *Empowerment* – Agile only works with a team that's 100% committed, and a team will only be 100% committed if all the members are 100% empowered. Let the team manage its work—your job is managing the project, not the team.

- *Openness* – all the team members can see all the projects. They can comment on other members' work, they can ask questions to understand their tasks better, and they can divide the work up between themselves.

Starting an Agile project

When you start an Agile project, you will divide the project up into several *user stories*. Each user story is a small piece of functionality. For an e-commerce site, for instance, it might be putting together an automatic discount facility on the shopping cart (10% off when the order goes above $50) or a recommendations service. For a marketing project, it might be a test direct marketing campaign. These stories become the *product backlog*.

Each story is delivered in one iteration so that the team is working on one thing at a time. This keeps the team focused on a single aspect of the project at a time. It avoids a common problem with large system projects, where teams have a highly diffuse workload and lack focus—and that can lead to problems not being spotted until a lot of time and money has already been committed.

User inputs, as well as comments within the team, are continuous. People don't go off and develop bits of code, and then come together on Friday to look at it—they are looking at each other's contributions to the project, and commenting, and helping, all the way through. You don't develop a whole great software system and dump it on the client at the end—you keep showing them how it is working, and they keep giving you feedback.

That is actually fantastic news for getting a good return on your project's investment. For instance, your client might have requested several user stories—a recommendations button, a search function, and a "tell a friend" facility. Suppose that the first two are delivering increased sales on the e-commerce site, but no one is using the "tell a friend" button—you can simply deactivate it or decide not to develop it further, not wasting money on something that isn't delivering what you expected.

Your team also works together continuously. For instance, many Agile projects use in-pairs programming. That can help deliver the next generation of Agile developers if you put your junior programmers in pairs with more experienced talent—it is what on-the-job training *ought* to be, delivering learning together with a business benefit.

Implementing Agile

So suppose you want to use Agile to manage a project. How do you start?

First, you want to define the project by reference to a business need or a product vision that your project will address. Basically: Why are you doing this project in the first place? You could simply spend the strategy meeting developing an elevator pitch—a one-minute pitch that says:

- who the project is for
- what they need
- what the product is
- the key benefit that your customer will get from it

Imagine one set of answers. "Our customer is the group finance department. They need a way to keep tabs on export contracts. We're building a searchable database, and they'll be able to see their days' sales outstanding by currency exposure, customer credit rating, and the customer's payment experience record—so they can manage currency and credit exposures." Or you might be developing a new stationery product. "Our customer is a 25-35 professional who does a lot of traveling. They need to keep their tablet, notepad, and travel tickets all in one place. We're going to design stylish travel luggage that meets these needs and will make their life much easier."

After you have defined your strategic vision, you then build the product road map. You are stacking up the basic requirements and adding a rough time frame. Focus on objectives; for instance, you might want to increase the number of customers or reduce days' sales outstanding. Add to these big goals the date you want to achieve them by, any features that are included in a product, and the metrics by which you will work out whether you have achieved your objective.

Now that you have got that in place, you can start working on more detailed timing. Obviously, there will be dependencies; you can't begin working out the costings for that travel luggage until you have a basic design. Work out the most important stuff to get done first. Now you are ready to kick off the project by planning each cycle of iterations.

You may also need to spend some time recruiting your team and ensuring you have the right resources. Having done that, get started on your first sprint!

Throughout the Agile project, you will want to have reviews. As soon as your first sprint has delivered a product or a project outcome, you'll want to have a review meeting. Keep it short, and avoid Powerpoint—a huge time waster. Check that the delivered product/outcome ticks all your boxes on the project plan. Talk about what the team has learned; were there things that went wrong, that can be addressed in the next cycle? Were there things that went right, techniques that you should formally adopt as part of the methodology, or ideas that might help deliver the project more quickly or at a lower cost? Agile is all about learning through continuous iterations, and the more you learn, the better your project outcome will be.

Remember: Move fast, deliver often, and keep responding to your users' changing needs.

The Benefits of Agile

Agile has several benefits as a PM methodology. For a start, you will get greater engagement from stakeholders, particularly customers. You will also be talking to your customers all the way through the project—not just at the beginning and end—and you'll be discussing the project fully with them rather than just giving a progress report.

This creates greater collaboration, but it should also deliver greater client satisfaction. If you are developing software, you will be delivering working pieces of software frequently, so the client can use them, evaluate the experience, and move on. Your client is getting value from the very first bit of software you deliver—not waiting until the end of the project.

Agile also delivers greater transparency for clients who are involved throughout the process. However, ensure the client realizes that what they are seeing is the work in progress—and that they don't expect every iteration to produce a bright shiny final product. And, of course, because the client is engaged, the project is almost certain to have a more precise focus on customer benefits—the benefits to users and the business overall.

Agile gives much quicker delivery than other methodologies. Sprints generally last from a single week to four weeks and are time-boxed, so something is being delivered at least every month. You can beta test, you can release early, you can release modules, but there's something useful being delivered. (Suppose you wanted to create a family of products rather than having a single project to deliver everything all together (the messenger bag, the backpack, the tote, the purse)—you could come out with one product at a time. That lets your customer test market rather than building up the whole family of products only to find they're not doing that well.)

However, the fixed schedule of sprints also helps to prevent cost/time overruns. Cost-conscious customers will be happy to know that the iterative nature of Agile project management also allows fine-tuning of the budget as the project proceeds. That would not happen in a more traditional PM approach. For example, you can increase the priority given to a software feature that really improves the customer's profitability (e.g., real-time tracking of customer orders), or you can reassess the costs of the next iteration given the last one came in 5% under budget.

Iteration helps with estimation. If you are trying to estimate from scratch how long it will take to deliver a certain product, it is tricky. You might come up with an estimate that's wildly off the mark. But if you have already carried out two or three similar tasks, you have a much better idea of the time required—and that feeling for what is involved in a given task will improve again as you keep going with the iteration cycles in your project.

Agile's use of a self-directing team empowers and motivates team members, but the idea that every team member can tackle any team task isn't just good for the team—since you are recruiting multi-functional individuals, there are no bottlenecks while everyone waits for the only team member who does product testing to be freed up. That is a huge change from other PM methodologies in which, often, each team member has a single given area of operations.

There are actually some interesting numbers on how much Agile can help a business. In 2009, Dr. David Rico compared Agile and other PM methodologies. He found that:

- 83% of Agile projects were more productive than non-Agile projects
- 83% had quicker time-to-market
- 50% were better quality
- 50% were less costly
- 41% showed better overall business value

The Six Deliverables of Agile

In terms of the paperwork for managing an Agile project, life is pretty simple. An Agile project can be summed up in just six deliverables:

1. *The product vision statement.* This is your "elevator pitch", lengthened. Who the product is for, what benefits it delivers, and, if relevant, what it replaces, or what it

competes against. You and the Product Owner will use this as your "Bible" throughout the project, checking that you're still doing what was intended and headed in the right direction. While you can revise the product vision statement, it probably doesn't need reassessing more than once a year—unless, say, a competitor brings out a new product that has a big impact.

2. *The product road map.* This is still a high-level statement, but instead of looking at what the product *is*, it looks at the requirements you need to deliver to achieve the product vision. All the major features that you need should be captured here. So, it might say: kanban board visualization; collaboration features; cloud computing implementation; Android/Apple/Windows/Linux versions. You might want to take a look at this every six months or so to ensure it's still exactly what you need.

3. *Product backlog.* This is the list of everything you need to do to carry out the project. You'll want to order it from high priority to lowest priority. This is about priorities, not about timing. What's the most important thing you need? Which features are desirable, but less important?—for instance, they might only apply to a small segment of your customer base, or they might be updates of something that already works but could be improved.

4. *Release plan.* This is your timetable for getting finished product out there. Don't forget that a working product is completely useless if you forget to release it to your customers! Up until now, your thinking has really been orientated towards the product. At this point, you need to start thinking more about your resources. What's the *velocity* of your project team? In other words, how quickly can they deliver software? Are there any dependencies you need to think about? How can you reconcile that with your customer's requirements for, say, a release at a particular major conference?

5. *Sprint backlog.* This is everything linked to the current sprint—user stories, goals, and tasks. This goes into much more detail. And at this point, the time pressure is on!

6. *Increment.* This is the working product that is ready at the end of the sprint. Whether it is a bit of software, or a product design, or a new process definition, it's there to be presented to the stakeholders and delivered to your customer… and then you can get started on the next sprint.

Of course, because Agile is iterative, when you have delivered your increment, you will be going back to the road map, the product backlog, and the release plan, and reassessing the plans. Can you release some product quicker? Have your priorities changed? This is where Agile really boosts your productivity—so don't miss this stage out! Some product managers think of the retrospective as "the seventh deliverable", and it is the one that makes the real difference between an Agile project and a traditional project. Make sure that you make the time available for reflection and for learning before you get stuck into the next sprint. If you like, this is the pause button—the point at which the busy Agile universe stops spinning for a moment, at which the time pressure is taken off, when you can breathe, and think, and learn, and make those micro-changes (and sometimes bigger ones), which will transform your project… and then you press the "play" button again.

Using a burndown chart

Within the project, you can look at where you have to in terms of sprints. That shows you whether your progress is up to expectations. But how do you track what is going on in a sprint? By using a burndown chart!

A burndown chart shows, over the course of the sprint, a daily total shown in work item hours. You can use the burndown chart to get a feeling for how well the team is performing and whether there are any risks or problems associated with the sprint.

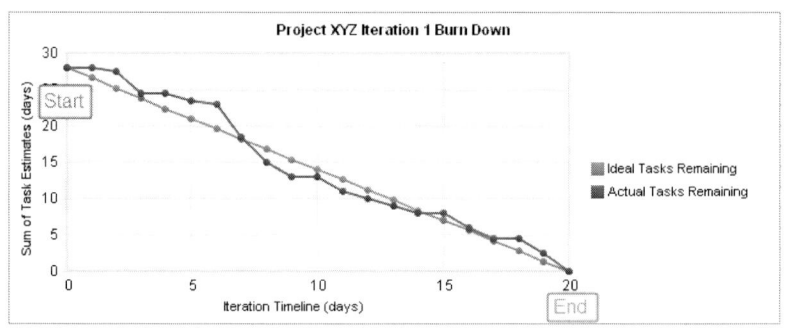

I8abug, CC BY-SA 3.0 <https://creativecommons.org/licenses/by-sa/3.0>, via Wikimedia Commons https://commons.wikimedia.org/wiki/File:Burn_down_chart.png

Of course, the simplest form of a burndown chart is a line that shows, each day, the total workload *less* the work that has been done—a steadily decreasing amount of work that remains to be completed. That is quite useful; however, what is even more useful to a Scrum Master is a burndown chart that shows the total workload divided into three categories—pending (backlog), in progress, and done.

A simple burndown chart for four weeks of an eight-week sprint. Here, the team is keeping work in progress stable, and completing it—but something went wrong, and there is more work in this sprint than they expected. Ideally, the total workload in all three categories will remain stable throughout the sprint. But it might not. In some sprints, the workload suddenly grows at some point. That is because the workload was badly estimated, and now the team has realized that there is more work involved than they thought. Or, possibly, the team has taken on new work. That is not a good sign—unless you can see that the "done" total has increased and given them some slack.

Work in progress should ideally be a fairly slim line. If the team is taking on too much work in progress, it lacks focus. A great big fat "work in progress" line is not good news. If at the same time, you don't see the bottom slice of "done" growing satisfactorily, then your team is taking on work but not completing it, and you need to start taking action. That is often something that happens early on in the life of a new Scrum team and ought to settle down after a few iterations. Introducing Kanban, with its focus on reducing work in progress, can help. If you can see a slim line of work in progress and it is trending upwards, that is, getting converted to "done" regularly, then your team is doing pretty well.

And, of course, you want to see that the "done" slice of work is increasing steadily. If the burndown charts show a team only completing half the work it took on, then there is a problem.

Remember, though, that the burndown chart is just a tool. It is a useful tool, but that's all it is. In the case of a team only completing half the work in the sprint, there might be several different reasons for that:

- It's early in the project, and the team didn't have a good idea of how much was involved in the work—hopefully, they'll adjust their estimation for future sprints. If the percentage of work completed goes up over the next few sprints, the team is learning—and that's quite normal.
- There was a particular difficulty that caused waiting time or that led to extra work or re-work. For instance, a major server outage meant that significant working time was lost in one week of the sprint.

Having too much work completed can be just as bad as too little. If a team manages to complete all its work for the sprint two days before the end of the sprint, they allowed too much time for the work to be done. For the next sprint, they will need to adjust to allow a bit less time; otherwise, you are basically giving everyone two days' extra holiday!

Scrum: All You Need to Know

Five values

Agile can be implemented with several approaches, including Kanban, Extreme Programming (XP), Adaptive System Development, or Crystal Clear. However, Scrum is the most popular, and it is an easy approach to implement. Remember, though, that it's a framework for implementing Agile methodology—not a methodology itself. It is also possible to use a blend of approaches—plenty of projects use kanban within Scrum, or XP techniques within Scrum.

The first thing you need to know about Scrum is the five values that it adopts. They are a bit different from much of what you will hear in more traditional project management circles:

- **courage,**
- **focus,**
- **commitment,**
- **respect,** and
- **openness**.

These values are not always easy to achieve—or to foster. Openness can be difficult when it involves having to confess to failure, or to say "I don't understand." Courage is often discouraged by corporate environments—the courage to say, "That's not going to work," or "You need to change this," for instance. If these values sound like they will make your kind of working environment, you'll be happy with Scrum, whether you are a team member or project leader.

Focus is also sometimes difficult. In many organizations, team members end up with a huge number of tasks all of which need to be done at the same time—for instance, a member of the finance team may be handling queries from different divisions at the same time as trying to revise monthly budgets and analyze business plans or sales orders that need finance sign-offs. Scrum enables focus through its use of sprints, which single-mindedly concentrate on getting a single stage of the process finished. (Using kanban, which will be looked at later, can make sprints even more focused.)

Commitment and respect sound easier values to incorporate, but remember that all the participants in Scrum need to show them—

that includes you! And commitment can be difficult for people who have, in the past, found that power politics has put them "in the wrong" for showing commitment to an unpopular project or manager, or that they have been asked to commit to unrealistic goals. Remember that you inherit team members who may not always have encountered the respect they deserve within the organization.

This is a good place to warn you against using Scrum just as a productivity-boosting method. Some companies try to use Agile and Scrum merely to up the work rate. They don't show much respect for the project teams. In some cases, managers pay lip service to Scrum but parcel out the tasks to team members themselves, instead of letting the team manage itself. If you, personally, can't commit a hundred percent to the Scrum values, then you should not be a Scrum Master—and you won't be a *good* Scrum Master. You won't make a great team member, either. A little introspection before you take on or decide to work on a Scrum project is always a good thing.

Three roles

In addition to the five values, Scrum has three fixed roles:

1. Product owner.
2. Scrum Master.
3. Team member.

The product owner, unlike the customer or sponsor of a traditional project, is continuously involved throughout the lifetime of the project. The product owner's role is to focus on business and market requirements, rather than just work that needs to be done; it is the product owner who is responsible for the product vision, and who keeps that vision to the forefront all the way through. While the product owner is not involved in the actual work of the sprint itself, they are involved in the sprint planning and sprint retrospectives, fine-tuning, and adapting the project in response to what has been learned and delivered by the last sprint.

The Scrum Master is a bit different from the traditional project manager. The scrum master's job is to be an expert on Scrum, to explain Scrum to the team, to stand up for the Scrum values, and ensure everyone is following the Scrum process. Scrum masters protect, lead, and enable their teams rather than "managing" the team. For instance, a scrum master will protect team members from having their work disrupted by questions from elsewhere in the business, and will ensure resources are ready when they are needed. Sometimes, team members may even need to be protected from a too keen product owner!

The reason that the scrum master does not manage a Scrum team is that the team is self-supporting. It is the team that decides on what tasks each team member does. The scrum master may need to facilitate, particularly in the early stages of a project, when the team is still beginning to gel, but the aim is to get the team to make its own decisions as much as possible. Once teams get a bit of experience, with a few sprints under their belts, they get better at estimating how much work is involved in delivering a particular outcome, and better at sharing it out and supporting each other.

A Scrum Team will include from five to seven members—a fairly small, full-time, nucleus. Usually, all team members are located in the same office; they are not distributed. (Some companies have adapted Scrum to work with telecommuting teams. That can work really well, but you need to put good hardware, software, and—very important—help desk resources behind your team so that glitches with basic technology don't screw up the sprint.) That is very different from the kind of distributed, multi-functional, very large project teams many people are used to in big companies.

There are no distinct roles in the team so that each member will be involved in a mix of work, and each member will discuss the work with other members of the team, comment on other members' work and invite others to comment on their work. There is no "representative" of a particular department, like finance or marketing. If you need sign-offs from other departments, getting them will be one of the sprint tasks, or it will be up to the Product Owner at the end of the sprint.

For IT people used to the defined roles of business analyst, programmer, and tester, this free-form team can be a challenge—but it can also be liberating and invigorating.

Scrum meetings

In most projects, meetings are based on a weekly/monthly schedule, or they are called in response to the project hitting particular milestones. Scrum is different. In Scrum, all the meetings are fixed, immovable meetings. These are:

- sprint planning,
- daily stand-up,
- sprint demo, and
- sprint retrospective.

At the **sprint planning meeting**, the product owner notes what features are a high priority. The team then chooses what they believe they will be able to complete in the next sprint. This is a collective decision—not one that is imposed on the team. The Scrum Master facilitates the sprint planning meeting, and it is time-boxed—it should last an hour, and that's it. (Time-boxes are one of the key features of Scrum and make projects work fast, but you need to be disciplined about keeping to the time-boxes. That means part of the Scrum Master's work as facilitator is sometimes keeping things moving along—stopping discursive digressions, pushing for a decision, stopping arguments about details that could be taken off-line, and making sure everybody is out of the meeting and back at work as soon as the minute hand hits the hour.)

At the start of a project, it can be difficult for the team to work out what they will be able to complete. A team that is starting out will need to calculate what they can do by looking at team availability. As time goes on, the team will have established its velocity, which can be ascertained by looking at previous sprints and the relationship between work accepted and work completed. So, at the start of the project, it is best to kick off with a sprint that people are pretty certain they can deliver with a bit of time in hand. Later on, less allowance needs to be made for contingency.

The scrum master will usually start the meeting by reminding everyone of the overall goal of the project. Then, the availability (and velocity) of the team is established, the definition of "done" is revisited, and any new information that could impact the plan is presented. After this, the backlog items are presented for the team to consider. The team can ask the product owner questions to clarify what is involved and to ensure the acceptance criteria for the user story are clear. If you are running this meeting, you will want to be careful to identify any dependencies that might affect the project and any concerns aired in the meeting.

The aim is to achieve a group consensus on the new sprint plan. If everyone agrees, then it is time to get back to work!

The **daily Scrum or daily stand-up** is a fifteen-minute meeting, first thing in the morning. It is held standing up so that people don't get too comfortable—the aim is to keep it very short and focused. It's a meeting to discuss the goals and any issues that have arisen. The typical questions are: "What did you do yesterday?" "What are you doing today?" and "Are there any roadblocks?" And that is it. Fifteen minutes is more than enough—spend more time on the Scrum, and you are stealing time that belongs to the project.

A good tip from one Scrum manager is if you have a kitchen timer, take it into the office and let it tick away during the Scrum. The ticking really focuses minds.

Reminding people how much time they have left is also useful— "You've got five minutes," "Only a minute left." That puts pressure on people to make the points they need to succinctly, and not waste time. Once you have worked with a Scrum team for a while, that gets easier—people get a good sense of just how long fifteen minutes is, and they get a feeling for what is important and what can be left unsaid.

The **Sprint demo**, in software projects, is a live demo of the software that is held at the end of the sprint. The team can see it working, discuss whether any fine-tuning needs to be done, and assess how it might affect future sprints. For another style of project, it might involve delivering a new product or process specification, or a product prototype. It's in this meeting that you see, basically, whether the Sprint worked—whether it delivered what it was meant to. This is an important meeting for the Product Owner, who can see what has been delivered, and how it fits into their product vision and road map.

If there are stakeholders concerned besides the Product Owner, they should also be at the demo. For instance, if you are trialing a new accounts module, you want to have the finance people who will be using it sitting in.

The demo should present the following information:

- the work that the team committed to delivering in this sprint,
- what was actually completed,
- key decisions made during the sprint, whether by stakeholders, the Product Owner, or team members,
- any relevant metrics (lines of code, etc.)
- a demo of the work itself (software, product design)
- a quick review of priorities for the next sprint.

The "key decisions" part is needed because Agile and Scrum are processes that incorporate change as part of the project. For instance, the team may have found that they needed to build in a link to a particular database, the Product Owner may have refined the marketing plan, or there may be a new cost requirement driven by the corporate budget process. These obviously need to be known so that the next iteration can take account of them.

How much time should you spend on the demo? That depends on the length of the sprint. For a one-week sprint, an hour is enough. You might add 30-45 minutes for each extra week so that a one-month sprint would get a three or four-hour meeting.

Following on from this is the **Sprint retrospective**. This is possibly the most important meeting of all, so don't miss it out! It is important because it's during the retrospective that the team pulls out any lessons learned, and thinks about improvements that can be made in the next sprint and during the rest of the course of the project. If you miss out the retrospective, you are not going to get the full benefit of either Agile or Scrum—the iterative nature of the process that makes continuous learning and improvement possible. The questions asked during the retrospective are: "What were the high points of this sprint?" "What were the low points of this sprint?" and "What improvements do we need to make, what roadblocks do we need to remove?"

The improvements made might affect the product vision, or might be improvements in methodology. Equally, members of the team might say that they need training in a particular technique or area, or that the team as a whole has a development requirement. It is important that the team takes care of its resource needs and develop *as a team,* as well as meeting the project requirements.

Very often, Scrum Masters decide to run the Sprint demo on into the retrospective without a break. That can work as long as you make sure that the Sprint demo is properly concluded before you start on the retrospective—that the Product Owner is happy with what has been delivered, that it works, and that there are no more questions to be answered or bugs to be fixed. You then need to change gear to think about *how* the sprint worked rather than *what* it delivered. (It's also a good idea if you say goodbye to the Product Owner after the demo. The retrospective is meant to be internal housekeeping, and no one on a project team wants to air their dirty washing while the customer is still around.)

The questions asked at a retrospective are:

- What did we do well in this sprint?
- What did we not do so well in this sprint?
- What is stopping us or blocking us from achieving our objectives?

Having quickly identified those areas, you can then move on to ask the important questions that arise from what you have found out:

- What things can we start doing in order to improve our performance?
- What things should we keep on doing?
- And what should we stop doing?
- How can we fix blocks—do we need more resources, a sign-off, a particular piece of equipment or software?

A good way to run your retrospective is to spend fifteen minutes just collecting the data. You might have one person writing down the topics on a whiteboard or three whiteboards labeled "good", "bad", and "blockers" on which everyone can write their feedback, or you might hold a discussion, or even use sticky notes on the table or wall. With good ideas, it is easy to decide to build them back into the process.

With negative information—the blockers and the things that negatively impacted the performance—, you then need to prioritize those ideas. For instance, what is the priority between "we need more training on the database capabilities" and "Jamie's code was full of holes this sprint?" One way to do this is to hand out Monopoly money to the team, every member getting an equal amount, and ask them to "buy" priority for what they consider the top issues to be addressed.

So, you now discuss the priority issues and work out whether you can fix them, or at least mitigate them, or whether, after all, you are going to leave them because they're just irritating but don't really affect performance.

If you are the Scrum Master, really listen out for personal issues in the team—you need to ensure they are resolved. Look for clues that someone's not saying exactly what they feel—you might want to have a chat with them outside the meeting, ask if there is anything wrong, and ask if there's anything you can do to help them with the next sprint. It could be, for instance, that they don't quite understand one of the new areas being addressed, but they don't feel able to admit that in front of the rest of the team. Or they may just not feel completely up to speed with the project and their place in it—sitting down to talk them through the Product Vision and Road map might be useful.

Remember the Scrum values? They are important when you're doing the retrospective. Small grudges or annoyances can sometimes fester—the retrospective is everyone's chance to tackle things that went wrong in a spirit of respect and openness. If someone didn't contribute as much as expected, team members need to talk about it. Was it because they don't feel confident in this particular area of the project? Is it training that they need? Have they been unwell? Did they feel under too much pressure? If the team as a whole feels that the project has gotten bogged down, this is the time to air that feeling—before morale hits bottom. The retrospective is a key meeting for the health of the project team as well as for the project.

At the end of each sprint, the whole team—not just the Scrum Master—meets with the Product Owner to prepare the backlog for the next sprint. That allows the priorities in the backlog to be changed, if necessary.

A great tip for managing a Scrum team is to set up a team wiki. It is a great place for information of all kinds, like:

- why the team decided not to fix a particular issue ("it would take too much time" or "it shouldn't affect the next five sprints, it's only an issue with this one")

- what is the definition of "done" (does it include testing? Documentation?)
- a detailed timeline of changes in the Product Vision and Road map

Agile Applied – Eight Best Practices

Every Agile project manager will tell you that there are some things you don't do—and other things that really work well. The following is a list of top tips for getting the best results, which has been compiled based on discussions with Agile Project Managers and Scrum Masters about how they manage their teams:

1. *Ensure the Product Owner understands their role in setting the vision and providing continuous feedback on how the project is succeeding.* The product owner needs to keep a tight focus on the product vision rather than getting bogged down with day-to-day project management. Remember to talk with them often about their overarching objectives and their overall vision. That's really important in keeping your project on track, not just in regards to the workload, but in terms of delivering the business benefit.

2. *Choose your team carefully.* Make sure all your team members understand the Agile approach and are committed to making it work. Try to ensure your team members are all multi-skilled so that all of them can take on any work package. (That might be difficult in some environments, but you need to try.) Keep the team tight and focused. Avoid pressure to "put someone from marketing on the team", for instance. Don't add extra team members you don't really need.

3. *Let your team manage itself.* Don't micromanage. Scrum isn't a command-and-control style project management framework—it's a framework that allows your team to learn and to apply that learning throughout the project. Guide the team, protect the team, and keep them focused

on the project vision. Provide the continuity, through the Scrum meetings, that they need to keep on track. And then let them decide how they're going to do the work, and let them get on with it.

4. *Don't skip sprint retrospectives.* If you do, you won't keep learning throughout the project, and you'll miss out on one of the biggest benefits of Scrum. The retrospective allows you to fine-tune the project as you work. It's only twenty minutes or so, but it's the most important twenty minutes in the whole project! Review what worked, what didn't work, how you can apply what you learned. Apply your learning points, and next iteration, you'll be talking in the retrospectives about how that worked, and whether you can do even better next time.

5. *Share the product strategy with the team even though they'll be concentrating on one sprint at a time.* It gives them a feeling for the flavor of the product and the way their work fits into the overall strategy. Every so often, you may want to revisit parts of the product vision with the team to ensure they're still clear about exactly how their work will be used.

6. *Clear the distractions.* During a sprint, team members should be focused exclusively on the sprint items they have been assigned. Ensure they're clear on exactly what's expected before the sprint begins, so there's no to-and-fro to clear up ambiguities or conflicts. And keep your Product Owner away from the team while they're working. (That's sometimes difficult with Product Owners who have been trained in a different environment—you may need to sit down and explain to them the benefits they're getting from Agile development, and the reasons they need to change their behavior.)

7. *Maximize learning opportunities, opportunities for feedback, and opportunities to adapt.* If someone has a

problem, don't just solve the problem; look at whether what you've done has applications elsewhere in the project, or whether it's a symptom of issues you can address in other sprints. Don't think about "problems" but about "opportunities for improvement".

8. *Have and give trust.* Agile only works when you trust your team, and when they trust the project manager. Some traditional project managers play politics with their team members—"divide and rule"—, but you can't do that in Agile. If the team stops trusting you, you're sunk.

It may sound easy, but it is not—or at least, it's not easy to do well. Scrum co-creators Ken Schwaber and Jeff Sutherland described Scrum as "easy to understand and difficult to master"—and that goes for any Agile implementation.

If you are producing software, you may also want to introduce some work methods from XP (Extreme Programming). That includes pairing, as well as:

- *TDD – Test-Driven Development.* You actually write the test before you write the code. The test defines a function, and then the code is written so that it passes the test. Writing the test requires you to understand what the user story demands *before* you start writing code. Software is then developed just to pass the test—not to do anything else. This can help provide focus and ensure you don't over-engineer the software. TDD also keeps the size of units small, again helping the team focus on just the single thing they're working on at any given time.

- *Code refactoring – improving the internal structure of computer code without changing its external behavior.* By continuously improving the design of the code, you make it easier and easier to work with. That helps to avoid the problem usually encountered when adding features starts to make the code unwieldy, and you spend more time integrating the new feature with the existing code than you do on writing the new feature. (You can sum it up as "tidy up as you go".)

- *Continuous Integration – merging all developers' work into a shared mainline code repository on at least a daily basis.* This helps spot problems early on, if you make the build self-testing. At the same time, it means that only small changes will need to be made to address any problems, reducing the amount of rework to be done.

Your development practices should be detailed in your project documentation or Scrum wiki.

Is Your Team Agile?

An Agile team is very different from most project teams. How can you tell if your team is agile? Here are a few ideas.

- What happens when you find out you're wrong? You learn. You adapt. You move on. If you get another answer—"we stop, we ask the product owner to help, we panic, we try to hide it"—, your team's not Agile enough.

- Halfway through the project, is the project plan still exactly what it was on day one? Or have you adjusted and fine-tuned it? If it's still set in stone, your team's not Agile enough. (Or you have a very unusual project!)

- If you have a whiteboard, everybody should be scribbling on it all the time. They should be adding their comments and commenting on what other team members have written. If the only handwriting on the whiteboard is the project manager's, your team's not Agile enough!

- Is software (or other product) going out every couple of weeks? If so, congratulations—you have an Agile team! If not, you're not achieving the desired velocity, and your team might need to work on its agility.

- When you come into the office, can you hear people talking? Are people often sitting together, looking at a single computer screen, or scribbling plans together? That's great. That's Agile. If the offices are strangely silent, with everyone sitting at their own desks all day, maybe your team needs to up its Agility.
- Can you change direction quickly if something's not working? If not… think about why. You need to become more Agile.
- In the current sprint, can you see how what was learned in the last Sprint has already been put to use this time around? Have your burndown charts got better and better as the team gets more experienced on this project?

And a few worrying signs that might warn you that you will need to do a bit more work on helping your team become properly agile: if

- half your team aren't located on site (obviously, this doesn't apply if you have a teleworking team);
- a member of your team is still reporting to another manager instead of the team;
- you hear, "I can't do that. It's not my area.";
- software is only tested when it's fully completed, just before it goes out;
- product you've completed has never been used;
- people don't turn up for the Daily Scrum;
- meetings run overtime by hours;
- you use a Gantt chart with all the project dependencies mapped out;
- team members communicate by email not talking;

- you never see the Product Owner; and
- the Burndown chart is more important than the Daily Scrum.

Common Agile Fails and Solutions

Thus far, a good amount of what you need to do to get an Agile/Scrum project motoring along has been covered. However, sometimes, Agile projects falter or fail. This is usually down to a fairly small number of problems. If you run through this list, you can easily see if you have got a problem that needs to be addressed—hopefully, before the project hits real trouble, rather than later.

- *Breakdown of trust.* In some Agile projects, the team members end up not trusting the project manager/Scrum Master or each other. You need to be transparent and to discuss all issues openly. People must feel safe to say honestly what they think, even if it's bad news. Sometimes, businesses introduce Scrum as a way of putting pressure on people to get product out more quickly—this can lead to a breakdown of trust, which needs to be addressed before the team can really work properly.

- *"Designing for conformity".* Being too prescriptive about the way things work can break an Agile project. Remember: Agile is about individuals. Some people love coding but hate documentation. Some people work fast, others in detailed mini-steps. Don't be too rigid. Let your team manage itself.

- *Not learning.* You need your retrospectives! Are the requirements poorly written? Can the testing not keep up? Are operations not pushing the releases out in a timely way? Learn, adapt, repeat. That's the essence of Agile. If you're missing out retrospectives, make sure you do them properly in the future. If you're not getting enough value out of them, work out why—not asking the right questions or not bringing the lessons learned back to the next sprint?

- *Output, not outcomes, focus.* When the focus is entirely on output—how many lines of code, how many products designed—, Agile doesn't do its best. It isn't just about "make more software more quickly"; it's about customer satisfaction and business benefits. If you're getting fixated on output, you need to get reacquainted with the product vision and keep telling your team about how their work fits in with it.

- *The product owner can't be bothered.* You need to have an engaged product owner, and they need to work with end users to manage their expectations and ensure your team doesn't just become everyone's favorite Santa Clause. They need to help you resist scope creep, keep refining the project, and keep the product vision in the forefront of everyone's minds. Their feedback is vital. Make sure you've got them on board.

- *It's all too much...* If sprints are not delivering the user story or if the team is getting frazzled, you might need to break the project down into smaller stories. (Again, learning from what happened and using that learning to adapt the project.) Use the iterative process to get each story delivered, bit by bit.

- *Wasting time on things that don't work or don't contribute.* You don't have to have meetings if there are only three of you, for instance (though it can help to focus, none the less!). Create your own PM process. If a particular process or technique isn't delivering, find another tool that works better, or just skip it.

- *Roadblocks.* Roadblocks appear in even the best project. Try to see where they might be ahead of time. You won't be able to foresee one of your team coming down with a cold, but you can think about what happens if resources are delivered late, or if there are approval requirements that could hold up work.

- *High friction tools.* This is where project managers coming from other PM environments sometimes come to grief. If there's too much reporting to do, team members will be wasting time on work that doesn't create customer value. Are you creating loads of data that's never going to be used? Are your reporting systems too complex and take too much time? Trim them down. If they don't add value, prune them.

- *Not releasing!* You don't get business value unless you release the software. Even if you're not responsible for the full implementation, make sure you know that the software is getting into the field.

You also need to apply Agile/Scrum in the right type of project. The Agile methodology prioritizes business value and product vision, and it works with small teams that are full time, or nearly so, and co-located. If you have a cross-functional project with many authorizations needed from different divisions, Agile might not work so well. Agile is great where you need flexibility and adaptation—but its advantages don't play so well where you have a set-in-stone product spec, such as on a single housebuilding project.

Agile needs a team that can function on its own, and most of the team members can handle most of the work. Where you have a lot of transient staff, where you have very large teams, or where your team is made up mainly of single-skilled staff, it's not going to be so appropriate. For instance, on a building site where electricians, carpenters, and masons all have very different skills and don't work on each other's parts of the project—sometimes, where they aren't even on site at the same—, Scrum isn't going to work at all. And it is difficult to use Agile for a single, all-at-once outcome like a big construction project (though on a multi-phase development, it might be a useful tool for the design team).

So, if your project does not feel like an Agile project, what can you do? Well, read on to the next chapter.

Chapter 3 – Lean Six Sigma

What is Lean Six Sigma?

This is a question that breaks down into two separate parts: first, what is lean, and second, what is Six Sigma? Adding the two together creates a project methodology, which is extremely good for handling projects that involve large volume processes—for instance, calls in a big call center, or a high-volume manufacturing process. It is targeted on waste reduction, so it's a great methodology to use in companies that need to reduce costs.

Lean

Lean is a methodological approach to streamlining processes in order to eliminate waste. Waste ("muda" in Japanese—you'll hear the term used if you work in a Kaizen environment) is defined as any work that does not add value. So, for instance, looking at several tasks that you might have if you were writing a book on project management:

- researching Six Sigma's history – adds value
- invoicing the publisher – adds value
- spending an hour trying to work out which of three Word documents is the current version – doesn't add value
- actually writing – adds value
- recovering work that wasn't backed up – doesn't add value
- looking at cats on the internet – doesn't add value
- completing a compliance checklist for the publisher's attorneys – doesn't add value

However, in that last case, ticking the boxes—that none of the work is plagiarized, that no specific instructions are given which might be considered actionable, and so on—is necessary, even though it does not add value. In a pharmaceutical company or bank or any other highly regulated industry, there is a lot of audit information that needs to be done even though it doesn't add value—so there is a special category for that. Lean doesn't demand you cut it out! That is called a business non-value add.

Astonishingly, in some businesses, the central processes consist of only 15% value add and 85% waste. That means 85% of the cost of your product or service does not contribute value to the customer. You could sell at much, much lower prices if you got rid of even half that waste.

Lean has seven categories of waste: motion, transportation, waiting, overproduction, inventory, over-processing, and rework.

1. **Motion** (of people). If you have to keep standing up, sitting down, or bending, that's a waste of physical resources. If you have to keep trotting between your office and a filing cabinet in the corridor or going up a ladder to get things off a too-high shelf, that's a waste. You could address that simply by relocating the filing cabinet or putting the more often needed items on a lower shelf.

2. **Transportation** (of assets). This might include a conveyor belt that doubles back on itself, needing to take things to another factory for the final fitting or having to move stock in and out of an inventory room. It can also include non-physical assets; for instance, if you have to post an email to eight different people to get a sign-off.

3. **Waiting**. Whether you spend two days waiting for approval from finance, or two minutes waiting for a bottleneck in the conveyor belt to be cleared, it's a waste of time. Bottlenecks are a huge source of waiting; you'll also find a lot of waiting involved where a process crosses divisional boundaries; for instance, moving from sales to finance, or from marketing to sales.

4. **Overproduction.** Often, businesses simply produce too much. For instance, sales might be going down, but you're still producing up to last year's budget. Overproduction is always waste. You might still be producing compliance data or reports that aren't needed anymore—that's a waste.

5. **Inventory**. In the just-in-time manufacturing universe, all inventory is a waste. It should either be being worked on right now or being sold. If you're in retail, obviously, you'll need some inventory—but keeping it as low as possible reduces waste.

6. **Over-processing.** British Telecom used to produce much of its own telecoms equipment, but it always seemed to cost more than competitors' products. That was because its engineers—very highly skilled perfectionist staff—kept adding features and improving the specification. Unfortunately, they didn't realize that what customers wanted was just a simple router—not one that could run a space station and two nuclear reactors at the same time as "whistling Dixie". It's over-processing when you add cost to a product without adding value.

7. **Rework** is the final waste. Whenever you get something wrong and have to remake it—resending an email that went to the wrong address, re-glazing the wedding cake that you misspelled the bride's name on, doing a new paint job on the car that was scratched in production—, it's rework. It's a waste. You could have been adding value instead.

If you find the list of seven a bit difficult to remember, some bright sparks have added an eighth type of waste, **Unutilized talent**, the waste of skills and people. It is a damaging kind of waste because not only does it have a straightforward economic cost, but it also demotivates your employees. For instance, where there is no career planning or progression, where people with advanced skills find they are spending most of their time on repetitive, unskilled processes (your highly skilled finance officer doing basic bookkeeping, or a doctor spending most of his or her time on allocating resources rather than patient care). Or where employees' good ideas are always ignored, you are going to find staff who are demoralized. That might also translate to higher staff turnover—another source of economic cost.

Why might eight be easier to remember than seven? Because there is a mnemonic, DOWNTIME, to help you (which is detailed later on).

Six Sigma

Six Sigma is a statistical methodology used to reduce variation and eliminate defects. It was first used by Bill Smith at Motorola but became much more widely popular after Jack Welch introduced it at General Electric (GE) in 1995.

Six Sigma is based on the concept of standard deviation. It looks at variation; that is, the range of difference between the average and the best and worst (greatest and least) values. So, for instance, you might look at how long it takes a waiter in a restaurant to take someone's order; the average might be just five minutes from the customer arriving, but the variation might be between one minute and 25 minutes. That is a bit worrying, as the customers who have been waiting 25 minutes are not going to be very happy. Six Sigma, in other words, shows you how much your performance varies.

Six Sigma then helps you solve these problems efficiently by looking at a bunch of data. A crucial figure is DPU, defects per unit; sometimes, it is expressed as DPMO, defects per million opportunities.

You will also have to work out your specification limits. How long *will* customers wait and still be happy? In a sit-down, mid-market restaurant, probably ten minutes or so—it would be a lot less in a fast-food restaurant. You can then identify the defects as every time that waiters don't take an order within ten minutes.

Now is the crucial factor that gives Six Sigma its name. Sigma, σ, is the mathematical symbol for standard deviation (the variation of a set of values). If you have a two sigma process, it is 69% defect-free. Increase that to three sigma, and you get 93% defect-free. At four sigma, 99%, and at six sigma, 99.9997% defect-free. That is your target.

So, you have Lean, which looks at waste, and Six Sigma, which looks at variability. They are slightly different approaches, but the idea behind both is similar; if you are delivering a product which is not predictable, has wide variances, or includes a lot of waste, you are spending much time and money on *not* delivering customer value. And if you can reduce the variances and cut out the waste, more of your effort will go to actually making your customers happy.

It is not surprising, then, that these two approaches can be used together as Lean Six Sigma. They have a natural fit.

Lean Six Sigma

Lean Six Sigma quite simply combines Lean philosophy with Six Sigma methodology. It can be used in any business to address rising costs and increasing competition. Its benefits include making processes faster, by removing non-value-added work—that might, for instance, mean creating a one-click ordering process for repeat e-commerce customers, rather than making them fill up a shopping basket. It will increase the quality of products and services by making them more consistent, and its strong focus on added value should result in increased customer satisfaction.

So, to sum up: Lean Six Sigma is all about removing waste—wasted materials, wasted effort, wasted time—and making your processes more consistent and reliable.

Waste: Explanation and Elimination Tips

Waste is defined as anything that does not create a product or service to the specification (and not over and above the specification). So, the first step in applying any Lean process is to identify your waste.

Don't do what many businesses do and waste resources by carrying out similar waste reduction projects in different departments! Keep your waste identification in a single repository—whether that is just a whiteboard in a small business or a full-scale searchable database in a larger organization. And make sure if you are starting a waste reduction project, that someone else just across the corridor isn't doing the same thing, and duplicating all the work you're doing!

Most waste in an organization occurs where different departments' responsibilities cross over. For instance, where finance requires sign-off for materials purchases, that can create waste as the manufacturing process is bottlenecked at some points. In many manufacturing businesses, when salespeople enter their orders, there is a whole load of waiting time, motion, and transportation as the order is transferred to the manufacturing and finance departments. Sign-offs may be required, the order may need to be broken down into different manufactured units, and, in some cases, the manufacturing department may need to clarify details of the order ("Yes, but it comes in white or black, which do they want?"). That is why you need to make sure any Lean Six Sigma process investigation is carried out across the entire business, not in a single department.

Having identified waste, you can then prioritize the worst areas of waste, those which are costing your organization the most money or time. You could also note those that are the easiest to fix—they're also worth doing even if the benefit is not very great. For instance, taking a very simple example of a single-person project, in a project manager's office, the following areas were identified and prioritized:

- *Motion* – all the important files were kept in a cabinet on the other side of the office. Every time they had to be consulted, the manager had to walk to the filing cabinet, get the file, and walk back. They added up the time—twenty minutes a day! High priority.

- *Rework* – because their software wasn't quite the same as one of the other department's, they spent an additional fifteen minutes or so every time they submitted a project making sure the presentations would show correctly on their system. Not a huge priority since that was only fifteen minutes a month.

- *Over-processing* – No one ever commented on the hours worked sheets that they distributed for the project teams they managed. When they asked, divisional managers said they didn't use the data, and it wasn't relevant to them. This was a relatively low priority, but it was very easy just to stop producing the relevant report and save a few minutes every week.

This might already be making you think about areas of waste in your office. However, add a bit of structure to help you assess waste more efficiently, in the form of a waste checklist. Run through this checklist, and you will spot a lot of wasted time, money, and effort; rate each form of waste according to the amount of waste and how easy you think it will be to eradicate and then prioritize the areas you want to tackle.

This checklist uses the DOWNTIME format that was referred to earlier. Use the headings to assess your process—remember: although much of the headings appear to refer to physical products, the concepts work for knowledge industries, too. For instance, an architect's office found that a lot of waste was connected to energy efficiency reports and data—waiting for consultants' reports, no central repository for energy-related information, and plans sent out without the required energy information leading to hold-ups in the planning authorization process.

DEFECTS – information, services, and products which are incomplete, inaccurate, or don't work:

- broken parts – if one component has a high failure rate, for instance
- missed deadlines – if they're recurrent
- incomplete products, whether that's missing a part, wrongly packed, or simply orders sent to customers that miss out some of what's been ordered
- incomplete forms – e.g., an invoice missing the PO number, healthcare forms that don't include the name of the patient's regular doctor, or forms that don't have vital consent boxes ticked
- misdiagnoses, software bugs – e.g., spreadsheets with missing links, or web pages with outdated links

OVERPRODUCTION – making too much of something faster than needed:

- redundant storage capacity
- too many copies of a report made

- continuing to produce a product for which demand is falling
- too much stock left at the end of the season
- one stage of the process is completing intermediate product before the next step of the process is ready to work on it, creating a "bulge" in inventory
- printing data out to file it in paper format!
- multiple copies of data that should be held only in a central repository
- non-standard processing

WAITING:
- waiting for sign-offs
- waiting for information to be provided
- waiting for equipment or components to be provided
- waiting for large batches to be completed
- system downtime
- maintenance downtime
- bottlenecks (QA system, packing)

NON-UTILIZED TALENT – not properly utilizing people's intelligence, skills, expertise, and creativity:
- skilled employees spending time on unskilled tasks
- time taken in paperwork about the job rather than doing the job
- employees who are not allowed to make basic decisions that they could easily handle (e.g., pricing when a regular mark-up applies)
- poor training, which prevents employees from doing a good job

- multi-skilled employees who use only one of their skill areas

TRANSPORTATION – any movement of materials, equipment, or information that does not add value:

- hand-offs between different functions
- resending and copying emails
- playing "telephone tag", messages getting shunted to voice mail and not acted on
- multiple reviews of the same product or decision
- product having to be moved between inventory and processing several times
- returns from customers
- poor design of work-flow

INVENTORY – accumulation of parts, finished goods, information, and applications beyond what is required by customers and adds value:

- stockpiling of physical product beyond what's needed to meet regular demand/seasonal peaks
- too much unused/unusable data being kept
- too much unnecessary information being created (reports, etc.)
- unused components
- overproduction of marketing materials
- food going to waste in a catering operation
- equipment that isn't used

MOTION – any movement by people that doesn't create value:

- need to walk between different equipment stations

- re-entry of data (e.g., a bank customer filling in their address when it could be pre-printed on the form)
- switching applications (when integration of systems could avoid this)
- repetitive keystrokes (e.g., need to tab in a form)
- people having to search for materials or tools
- hand-offs in software development
- repeated bending or stretching—could have an impact on employee health and nonattendance rates
- calling distributed staff into unneeded meetings

EXTRA-PROCESSING – any steps that do not add value *in the customer's eyes:*

- information that's not requested or useful
- extra features that don't differentiate the product ("over-engineering")
- marketing touches that don't add value (e.g., personally delivering products; gift wrap for non-gift items)
- ordering unnecessary tests for patients, or prescribing unnecessary medication

Note down each type of waste that you see and categorize it as a high, medium, or low rate of waste. Describe the issues ("software requires three authorization steps to be completed where only one is needed," "testing station is too far from production equipment, so staff spend time walking back and forth"). Then sit down, ideally with your team or with another colleague, and assess which sources of waste really need to be addressed, and which sources of waste are an easy fix. If you are really fortunate, you will find some that are *both* big sources of waste *and* easy fixes, so that gives you an excellent place to start!

What you have not done yet is to adopt any of the different Lean Six Sigma methodologies for quantifying this waste and assessing a process through Value Stream Mapping. This will be detailed in the next two sections. If you run Lean Six Sigma, you need to get happy using calculations and statistics because there is a lot of that going on—particularly in the pure Six Sigma stuff where you are aiming to make processes more standardized and reliable.

However, just running through this list without applying the full LSS methodology and using the various tools is still a useful way to identify and eradicate waste. If you work in a small business, you may not need to go any further for the time being—but if you have a complex process in a larger corporation, you probably want to go further. The more complex processes become, the less likely it is that you are going to take the optimal action by just acting on one step in the process, and the more you're going to need the methodological and statistical backup of full Lean Six Sigma project management.

Tools and concepts for Lean Six Sigma

Once you really get into Six Sigma, you will find that you want a few extra techniques in your toolbox for analyzing waste and how to eradicate it. These are a few of the most commonly used techniques; each one is explained so that you can use it easily. Additionally, you should read the kanban section later in this book—kanban is a powerful tool to use within Lean Six Sigma, as well as in Agile, or indeed in any business or project management process.

Punchlist

A punchlist, also called a snag list, comes from the construction industry, but it is useful in any project. It identifies aspects of the project that are incomplete or deficient, or that need to meet certain compliance standards. It contains all the relevant deadlines, expectations, specifications, and assignments. It's your go-to document for checking that tasks have been completed.

The most important feature of a punchlist is that it is not just a list of tasks; it has an action history attached, so any member of your project team can easily see where you have got to at any given moment.

Pareto diagram

The Pareto principle is also known as the 80/20 rule. It says that 80% of the effects come from 20% of the causes. For instance, 80% of your sales volume comes from 20% of your products; 80% of your waste comes from 20% of your process failures.

A Pareto diagram sums up the causes and effects of waste so that you can see where your project's effort will be best applied. The left vertical axis shows you the frequency of problems or the total cost of process problems, so that gives you a bar chart showing each problem as a bar. The right vertical axis shows the *cumulative* frequency or cost of these problems, drawn as a line.

You can use that line to give you a cut-off point for your project. For instance, if you want to reduce the cost of poor quality by 50%, follow that line to the 50% point, draw a line down to the vertical axis, and then see what bars are on the left of that line. If you address those problems, you will have halved the cost of poor quality. There will probably be only three or four big problems that side of the line, while there might be seven or eight smaller ones on the other. Basically, the Pareto diagram is a way of prioritizing your project so that you get a bigger bang per buck.

Why-why-why diagram

The why-why-why diagram is a "tree" chart that is very simple to use. It's really powerful if you use it on a whiteboard as a way of working with a process team to analyze their problems. You start at the top with the problem—orders are getting delivered to the wrong addresses. Then you ask "Why?"—so perhaps you have several answers: incomplete address information, subcontractor error, or customers with more than one business address.

Why-why-why – some people prefer to call it "5 Y's". Think of the way a three-year-old keep questioning—why, why, why, why, why? They have a point. Usually, a parent's first answer is just a way of getting the child to stop talking—they have to ask again to get a real answer. In business, often the first answer to "why" won't get you to the root cause—it will just deliver a symptom. So, you need to keep asking "why" until you get to the root of the matter.

1. **Why** were these products returned? – because they're not built to spec.
2. **Why** aren't the products built to spec? – because the salesperson phoned the order through instead of entering it into the system.
3. **Why** did the salesperson phone the order through? – to get hold of the production manager.
4. **Why** did they need to get hold of the production manager? – because the order was too big to enter into the system without the manager's sign-off.

Aha. You have a system that works well for small orders, but the big orders have to get authorization, and therefore, they bypass the system that works. You need to make sure all orders go through the same system, perhaps with an optional breakout loop for the big orders. In this case, it took four "why's" to get to the real root of the problem.

You draw the tree, giving each of these answers a box. Then you ask "why" again. Why are addresses incomplete? Answers might include: not enough characters in the data entry field, poor handling of telephoned orders, or address stickers start to come apart when wet. Now add those answers to the tree, and ask again for each of them: "Why?"

You may find there are duplicate causes in several of the branches of the tree. You may also find it is easy to spot the key cause. Or you may need to carry out more research to find out which of the causes you have identified is the major culprit.

Fishbone diagram

Also known as an Ishikawa diagram after its inventor, the fishbone is another great tool for analyzing the causes of problems. It is similar in some ways to the why-why-why diagram, but instead of drawing a tree, you are drawing a fish. It is really useful for brainstorming.

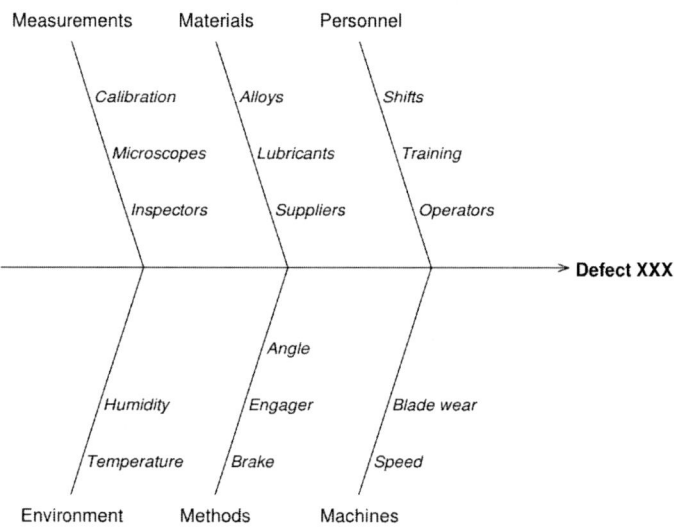

DanielPenfield, CC BY-SA 3.0 <https://creativecommons.org/licenses/by-sa/3.0>, via Wikimedia Commons
https://commons.wikimedia.org/wiki/File:Diagrama_d%27Ishikawa.png

Start with the fish head on the right—the problem. "Website downtime". Then draw the backbone and the first pair of fishbones. "Electricity supply issues" might be one, "can't connect to server" another, or "DNS issues" or "hardware failure". Along each fishbone, write the lower level possible causes; for instance, "can't connect to server" might have "overloaded server", "firewall", "software issues".

Having used the fishbone diagram to identify possible causes, you now need to think of ways of verifying what causes are affecting your process and quantifying the impact of each.

Takt time

Takt time is the maximum time you have to produce your product or service and meet customer demand. It is calculated by taking total available time (less staff breaks, shift changeovers, and maintenance downtime), divided by customer demand, for a particular period (day, week, month).

Look at your current cycle times against takt time. If your cycle is much faster than takt time, you may find the work could be rebalanced among fewer operators or using fewer resources. Of course, you may need to allow a buffer for peak demand—there is no single "right" answer!

The takt time concept addresses overproduction as a form of waste—you may be providing product much more quickly than you need to.

Correlation Chart

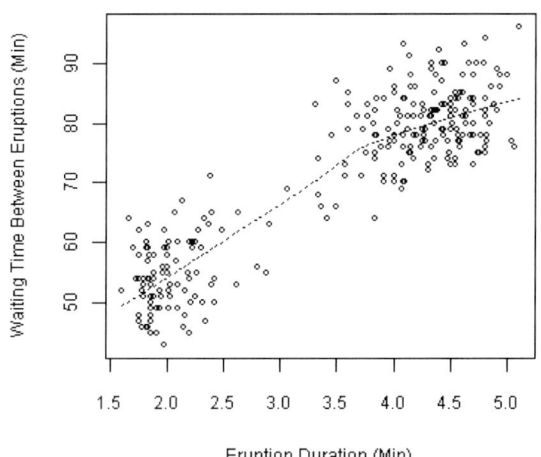

https://commons.wikimedia.org/wiki/File:Oldfaithful3.png

A correlation chart shows the relationship between two variables as a scatter plot. For instance, you might plot downtime against the age of machinery, to see whether the two are correlated. A huge advantage of a correlation chart is that it is easy to assess visually—if the plotted points cluster around a line, you can see the correlation, whereas if they are widely scattered around the chart, the two variables are not related.

In the latter case, then, you can forget about updating the machinery in order to improve reliability—something else must be responsible for the downtime. (That might be lack of maintenance, operator error... you can probably think of more.) And even if there is a good correlation, it doesn't always indicate causation; for instance, apparently, the age of Miss America correlates with the number of people murdered by steam, hot vapor, or hot objects, but do you really think Miss America is responsible? So, you will need to do more analysis and testing to work out if the chart shows a real cause or just an accidental correlation.

Watch out—another reason two variables *might* be correlated is that there is a third common cause involved. For instance, your web server downtime might correlate with false alarms from your burglar alarm—neither is causing the other, but power cuts could cause both of them!

Value Stream Mapping Hacks You Should Know

To implement a lean management process, your first step is to draw the business process. That might be simple—take customer order, make sandwich, pack sandwich, take money, hand over sandwich—or it might be considerably more complex. However, as well as just drawing the flow chart, you need to include metrics, such as cycle times, waiting times, defect rates, and value added. It is this information that you can use to identify waste.

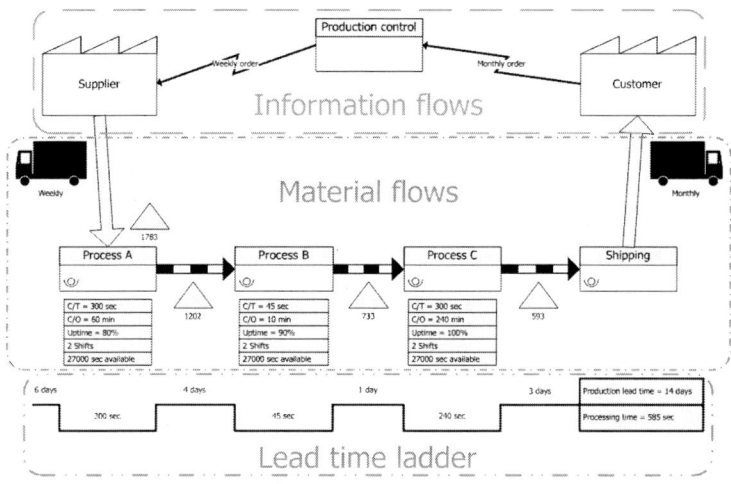

A value stream map example. DanielPenfield, CC BY-SA 3.0 <https://creativecommons.org/licenses/by-sa/3.0>, via Wikimedia Commons https://commons.wikimedia.org/wiki/File:ValueStreamMapParts.png

Collecting those metrics can be tricky. The business might not collect all the data you want. And sometimes, processes have "hidden" parts that only two or three employees know about and that aren't in the job manual. But if you go about the mapping properly, you will end up with a total map of the value stream in your business, and you can use that to identify waste and the cost of that waste.

"Value stream" will now be defined because value stream mapping is a bit different from the flow charts of process mapping that most people are already familiar with. A value stream is a series of steps that occur to provide the customer with a product or service. Value stream mapping shows the steps in the process not in terms of decisions (go/no go) or individual tasks (mix the salad ingredients, add the dressing), but in terms of where value is added—and where it is not.

Looking at a value stream map helps prioritize where you can reduce waste. It is also useful because, sometimes, you need to optimize a total process to make a difference—not just one part of the process. Having a value stream map means you can look at the whole process, and clearly see the impact a chance on one step will have on other parts of that process.

Without value stream mapping, for instance, you might concentrate on reducing the inventory levels in part of the business. However, if you have a value stream map, you will see that beyond a certain optimum level, reducing the component inventory would lead to waiting at two other steps of the process, and would prove counterproductive.

Here are some good tips that will make value stream mapping much easier:

- Be really clear about what process you're mapping. Use a Pareto analysis or other data analysis methods to work out what processes are the most important. If you try to map every process in your department, you're going to do a lot of work before you get any return—if you map the one that's the most important or most costly, you'll get a better payback.

- Know where the process begins and ends—that might be with raw materials at one end and the customer at the other, or the salesperson taking an order at one end and the warehouse getting a picklist at the other. This gives you the boundaries of your map.

- You don't need to break the process down into single tasks—just show where the inventory or information needs to go (production line, stockroom, finance function) and when it enters and exits.

- Use sticky notes and a really big whiteboard to create your map. Sticky notes are easy to add and move around if you find they're in the wrong place. And use a big board because value maps always end up bigger than you think they're going to.

- Don't do it on your own. You need a team to do value stream mapping properly, and it should include everyone involved in the process. You might even include customers (particularly in a B2B business, like an auto parts maker supplying major auto companies) and external suppliers.

- Don't allow scope creep. Be clear on the value of the project and what you're aiming to deliver; otherwise, the project itself will have waste built into it! So, if you're going to look at the process of making those sandwiches in the shop and not at stock levels, don't get drawn into "who orders the materials and how much should we have" discussions. (Although, in this case, you might find the discussion of the materials is the one you should be having first because it's probably responsible for much more waste than the sandwich ordering-to-handover process in the shop.)

- Pick processes that matter! Get started on processes that are central to your business. That might be the basic manufacturing process; in transport, the ticketing process because that impacts your customers. Or it might be processes that link to your strategic plan, such as the software development process in an ERP provider (rather than, say, the process for booking salesforce appointments or buying hardware).

- Get quick wins. Focus on a single aspect at a time, sort that out, then move on. How do you eat a whole elephant? Answer: one bite at a time!

- Experiment. Once you've done your analysis and worked out how you can improve your process, run a pilot or trial before you move to full-scale implementation. That might involve using just one of several production lines, piloting a new process for a week before assessing it or rolling out a new software process in one bank or agency branch. That way, if there's anything you've overlooked and the new process doesn't work as you expected or delivered the benefits you'd identified, you can discontinue it.

- Get buy-in from employees by delivering for them, too. Find out what makes their lives difficult—do they hate multiple sign-ons? Is a particular bottleneck a source of irritation? Or is the layout of the office bugging everyone? These projects might not be about those important processes that affect customer interactions or your strategy, but very importantly, they will get everyone on board. Personnel quickly see that your projects can make their working lives much easier and more rewarding, rather than being just yet another demand on their time.

- Be clear about which are the key metrics. You may be fortunate enough to have access to a vast amount of data, but that blessing can be a curse in disguise if you can't see the wood for the trees. Which metrics are *really* useful? Don't track data that isn't significant. Keep measurements simple and simple to track—and help everyone throughout the business to track them. (One beer festival has three key metrics—people through the door, beer drunk, money spent—but makes them really powerful by letting everyone have the numbers within half an hour of the doors closing. That means re-ordering, selecting beers that need to be sold at a discount, and other profit-optimizing actions can be taken quickly.)

- Reward your team. Make it fun. Celebrate a new process rollout with a pizza dinner. Have a sweepstakes on how much waste you can save in the first month of a new process. Think of ways to keep people engaged. Just because it's a serious project doesn't mean you can't enjoy yourselves.

Adding the data is where good value maps really excel. The following looks at the kinds of data you need to add.

Inventory data is important because excess inventory can be a huge source of waste. Be careful to check physical inventory as well as what's on the database; sometimes whole pallets of inventory get "forgotten" in a storeroom or tucked away in a corner. Sometimes inventory was called off for a rush order, not used, and then left where it was instead of being returned to the stockroom.

Cycle time tells how long the process takes. There are two kinds of time; actual processing time and lead time—how long it takes for a given product to go through the system, including waiting, inventory, transportation, etc. Often, you will find that the actual processing takes a few minutes, but the lead time is weeks! The difference is, of course, waste. Squeeze the difference between the lead time and the processing time, and you're reducing waste while also making the process able to deliver a finished product to the customer quicker.

Uptime and downtime need to be added to the map. If there's high downtime on equipment, that can translate to a lot of waiting and long lead times.

(A nice little story here shows that some people appreciate the value of uptime. One brewery had two bottling plants, one installed in the 1980s and one installed back in 1950. The finance director had managed to set aside enough money to buy a new plant and was about to replace the 1950's machinery when a junior produced a value map he'd worked on. The downtime on the 1980's machine was 30%. On the older machine, it was just 4%. It was much more reliable, having been built by a better manufacturer and well maintained, while the 1980's plant was lower quality and had been bought secondhand from a business that had used it pretty hard. Result: the *newer* machine went to the scrapyard!)

Setup times are important in manufacturing, where machines may need to be switched over to a different setting for different products. For instance, if you're using CNC lathes to produce premium fountain pens, each new model will require a separate setup. If the set-up time is just a few minutes—for instance, if you have a computer program with all the parameters already set—, you can handle quite small batch sizes efficiently. On the other hand, if all the data points need to be entered separately, you may find that the set-up time is five or six times longer than the actual production time. That could be a big issue.

Rework and the **cost of poor quality** should also be entered on the value stream map. For instance, if 8% of the cupcakes you bake are rejected as misshapes or because they've burned, that goes on the value map and shows you where you have a waste in the process that can be reduced. If software is sent back for recoding, again, that's a value that needs to be entered.

Once you have completed a value stream map, you have a document that gives you all the important information about the process you've mapped. It shows the state of play right now. You can use it to work out where there is waste (lead time, waiting, etc.) that you could take out of the process. You can also use it to model the results of possible waste reduction actions and see how they work over the whole process.

DMAIC vs. DMADV

Lean Six Sigma has two key methods for operating an improvement cycle: DMAIC and DMADV. Depending on what kind of business you are in and what kind of project you're running, one will tend to be more appropriate than the other.

DMAIC has five stages:

- **Define** your project definition and scope,
- **Measure** the baseline performance of the process,
- **Analyze** the data and process flow to determine waste, defects, and variation,
- **Improve** by finding solutions, and
- **Control** to sustain the gains by monitoring the process improvement.

You can run DMAIC through many iterations. Each time, the control data from the last project will become your baseline data for the new project. The key is that data—finding Key Performance Indicators (KPIs) that give you a handle on how the process is working and whether there is still waste that you can get rid of.

DMADV—also known as DFSS, "Design for Six Sigma"—also has five stages. The first three steps are the same, but the last two stages are:

- **Design** the new product or process, and
- **Verify** that it is acceptable to all stakeholders, meets the specifications, and delivers the benefits expected.

In **Define**, you will want to assess what the business problem you are aiming to fix is, or what the product or process that you want to put in place is. For instance, you might look at the fact that customers are waiting too long to talk to your call center. Your aim is to reduce this waiting time. You might have some customer research that gives you a feel for what waiting time customers are prepared to put up with.

You want to be specific about the scope of the project. Your project charter document should sum this up, together with some other basic information—who is the customer for the project, what outputs are critical, what resources you have projected, and the estimated timeline.

Having got all of that straight, you can move on to the **Measure** part of the process. Good data is the beating heart of Six Sigma, but you will need to think hard about what measurement to use and how it is recorded. For instance, you might find that times are not always automatically recorded, or that while initial wait times are recorded, if customers are put on hold, there is no check on how long they wait after that point. You may need to specify new systems of measurement. Other measurements you could use include inventory amounts, customer returns, rejected products… and so on.

For a DMADV project, you won't have measurements within the business, yet, but you can use benchmarking, market data, and other external data to provide a basis for your project analysis.

Measuring helps you to establish your baseline and will also help you do your analysis. Remember: You will also need data for the Control/Verify phase of the project, so you need to ensure that data collection policies are built into the specification. Otherwise, you might have a great project but no way of checking that you have achieved the project goals.

Once all the measurements are in place, move on to **Analyze** what you have. Look for the root cause, using the "Five why's", brainstorming, interviews with people working in the relevant area, value stream maps, and other techniques, as well as using the data you have collected.

You probably have several possible causes for the problem or waste. Select the three or four that seem most likely. Now, you are going to become a process detective. You will want to think about what information will establish which of those causes is the guilty party. Just as the detective might look for fingerprints, bloodstains, check out alibis, and so on, you need to think about what data would establish which process inputs are responsible for the failed/wasteful outputs.

It is crucial to think your way through the analysis properly and not jump to conclusions; otherwise, you could waste effort changing the process or designing a new product but not actually getting the expected business benefits.

Once you are certain you have done your analysis properly, the road forks. For DMAIC, move on to **Improve**. Identify improvements and then test them. Measure the results. Take feedback from staff involved in the process: Was it easy to implement? Did it have the expected effects? Were there any knock-on impacts on other parts of the process or business?

Try to find ways to pilot or test-run a solution. For instance, you might run two processes in parallel using a common database, or you might run an initial direct marketing campaign to a small slice of your customer list. And once it is ready, roll it out properly.

Finally, **control.** Follow up the implementation, monitor the data, and make sure the benefits are being received. You may need to back up the process changes with training for some of the staff, or with additional fine-tuning. Watch out for the tendency to revert—sometimes things start well, but then people start to get slack, and the KPI starts to slide back towards your baseline. That is a bit like starting really well on your diet, but after a month or two, you find packets of chips and bars of chocolate magically reappear in your shopping basket.

The control stage of the process is not just a "police" stage; it is the part of the project that ensures your changes are sustainable—that makes the change "stick" and beds it in properly. If you just plant a tree and never water it or give it fertilizer, you won't get good fruit; in the same way, if you implement a process change but don't control it, you won't really get the benefit. Make sure your changes are well and truly bedded in before you close the project.

For DMADV, analysis is slightly different as you will be looking at benchmarks. You'll be defining the market or designing scorecards, and developing design concepts or alternatives. You'll want to do some thinking about the total life cycle cost of a design, not just the running cost.

After analysis, you will move on to the **Design** stage. You are aiming to develop new processes—using brainstorming, benchmarking, and value stream maps to come up with new solutions. For products, this is the stage at which you'll prototype a more detailed model of your selected design. Once you have designed a few different processes, take a good look at them and select the best. Focus on the easiest and lowest cost solutions—there is always a more difficult and costlier way to do anything, but with luck, that's the route your competitors will take!

Finally, you will implement your design and **Verify** that it hits the spot. Is it acceptable to all the stakeholders? Does a pilot marketing campaign show that consumers are willing to purchase your new product at the right price? Does the process deliver all the benefits you expect?

As well as verifying, you need to document all the lessons learned. The knowledge and experience you accumulated on your project journey are not useless once the project is over—they will be useful for the business in the future, so make sure you have a good closing document written up.

Throughout both DMAIC and DMADV, you will be working in a PDCA cycle—Plan, Do, Check, Adjust. (Confusingly, it's also known as PDSA, the Deming wheel, or the Shewhart cycle.) Every single thing you do needs first to be planned, then tested, then monitored, and adjusted and fine-tuned in the light of what you find out. Get used to thinking "PDCA" all the time about everything you do, and you will add value to even the smallest project actions.

How to Apply Lean Analytics

Lean Analytics gets a bit nerdier and more numbers-orientated, and if you are not someone who was a math whiz at school, you might find it hard going. However, Lean Analytics is really useful for getting your processes racing fit, particularly in startup companies and in sales and marketing processes. If you're in e-commerce, you *need* Lean Analytics.

Crucial to lean analytics are two factors:

1. iteration – repeating the cycle of building, measuring, and learning, then adapting to take account of that learning; and
2. metrics – working out what is the key metric that determines your success, and making sure you monitor it.

Where lean analytics differs from most Six Sigma implementations is in the accent on speed. It is Six Sigma done in high gear! The building, measuring, and learning are all done in really fast iteration.

For instance, an e-commerce startup may decide to use small tests of 500 direct marketing emails at a time. It will measure the response rate—a simple and effective metric. As it keeps testing, it drops the emails that generated a disappointing response rate, and it runs more of the emails that got the best response. Constant experimentation goes together with lean analytics to create a fast-moving and fast adapting business.

Simple metrics

Vital to Lean Analytics is not overthinking or overcomplicating your analytics. Only one metric will matter at a time. For instance, if you are trying to get your product known, and build a customer base, you're probably going to want to look at response rates. If your product is getting known, but you want to give it a big sales push, you might want to look at conversion rates instead. You could use any of the different metrics that web analytics can deliver:

- click-through rates,
- unique visitors to your website,
- average user time spent on the site,
- customer acquisition cost,
- average transaction value,
- conversion rates,
- churn,
- revenue per average customer,

but you are going to focus just on one metric at a time. Of course, the beauty of using fast iterations is that if you want to move on to focus on another metric, you can do so really easily.

Outside the internet world, you can still look at key metrics. For instance, a great metric for restaurants is staff to revenue—it gives you a feel for whether the staff is run off their feet (and customers are waiting too long), or whether you have too many staff on a slow night (and are burning through money). Keep it simple!

Data by cohort

One thing that is often missed is the fact that all customers are not the same, and their experience and behavior can be very different, depending on when they started using your product or service.

- The early adopters, customers who used your service when it was new, may not have had a great experience. They may be moving on to other newer products by now!
- If you had a big product redesign after six months, customers whose first experience was of the new product might be

much happier, and might order more of it, or more frequently.

So, it is worth slicing up your metrics according to time-slices to get your customer "cohorts".

What order to do things in

Lean analytics suggests that starting a tech or retail business has several stages, and it helps if you do them in the right order. That, in turn, will suggest what metric you should be using at each stage of the process. The stages succeed each other like this:

1. empathy – understanding the customer's needs
2. stickiness – creating something they'll want to use over and again
3. virality – getting customers/users to promote your product for you
4. revenue – monetizing your product
5. scale – increasing the scale on which you operate and getting scale economies

So, in stage two, stickiness, you will want to make sure your website has content that customers want to keep looking at. That might be products, or it might be advice, forums, or pictures of cute kittens. If you try to get to virality without getting stickiness, you'll get many more users, but they won't stay very long—you missed the goal. And you need to get both stickiness and virality in place before you try to monetize your product, or you won't have enough sales to pay your development costs.

Measuring each stage needs the right metrics. Your metrics will be about dwelling time—how long users stay on the site. With virality, you will want to measure social shares, inbound links, shares to clicks, and impressions to shares. Once you get to revenue, you are looking at conversion data, average transaction value, and so on, and once you get to scale, you're going to be looking much harder at transaction values in terms of upselling.

Mastering Lean Six Sigma Roles

Lean Six Sigma has different roles, and it is rather more structured as you might expect from what you have already read about it.

Lean Six Sigma projects may use both external and internal resources; external consultants or customer representatives, for instance, as well as internal team members. Internal resources are not required to have expertise in Six Sigma, but deliver functional expertise in their area—for instance, database management, or factory floor production.

The Sponsor has a vital role. It is the Sponsor who provides the budget or resources and actively supports implementation. The Sponsor needs to be at the executive level and has infrequent contact with the project personnel. It's the Sponsor who ultimately owns the process and is the final decision-maker. The Sponsor has limited involvement with project operations but is sometimes the person needed to remove roadblocks or secure additional resources.

The next role is the Champion, usually a mid-level manager, who has a much more frequent involvement with the project. The Champion leads the culture change and controls the process within their department. The Champion gives resource and management buy-in to the project, and can often help remove blockers, and secure resource. The Champion should be meeting with project leaders at least every couple of weeks.

Finally, the Process Owner is usually a manager or supervisor, who directly owns the process, drives coordination, and is in very frequent communication with the project personnel. The Process Owner can escalate issues to the Champion if required but doesn't usually have a budget or significant extra resource. It's the Process Owner who will implement the solution, and take over and control the improved process at the end of the project.

Subject Matter Experts fill support roles as required. Their communication with the project is ad hoc and depends on the project's requirements. They may be used as data collectors or business process experts, and usually, they don't see the bigger picture of where the project fits in the business. They, therefore, don't have the same level of ownership as the Sponsor, Champion, and Process Owner.

Lean Six Sigma also has roles for project-specific personnel who are not part of the process itself. They are given titles, which come from the Japanese martial arts—green belts, black belts, and master black belts—depending on their level of experience and expertise. They act as project leaders, teachers, and mentors to their teams, and deliver a solution to the process owner. Black belts are dedicated to the project full time, but green belts may work part time. Green and black belt certifications are gained through training courses and experience on LSS projects.

Green belts will tend to manage shorter projects that are more limited in scope. Usually, the project is in their functional area (e.g., marketing, finance) and doesn't cross divisional boundaries.

Black belts work on larger projects with longer time frames, which might be from three to six months. These projects often extend across functional areas. Sometimes, a black belt will work on a green belt led project as a mentor—LSS applies much thought and care to training and mentoring. Master black belts may manage multiple projects and also manage black belt training within their organization.

Where to use Lean Six Sigma

LSS is a particularly good project methodology for companies that are concentrating on low-cost and consistent delivery, and for analyzing continuous processes, such as manufacturing, sales, or human resources within a larger organization. It is very useful for large scale services—for instance, it can transform the efficiency of large call centers. LSS works well where you have people working full time on a single process.

LSS is less relevant where your business has a large number of customized one-off products and services. It is less relevant if you don't have the kind of business that has multiple data points. If you haven't traditionally tracked process data, you may have to start thinking about new measurements and data points before you can put LSS in place. It can also be difficult to implement where many of your staff work on multiple different processes at the same time.

Lean Six Sigma is also less relevant to startups and fast-growth companies, though lean analytics is a very useful way to look at managing tech startups—this only scratches the surface here, so if that has aroused your interest, be sure to look up the reading suggested in the Resources chapter.

By the way, do not reject LSS because you think you don't have time for a Lean Six Sigma project. If you are a small business and you're run off your feet, Lean Six Sigma might help you work out the reasons why!

Chapter 4 – Kanban and Kaizen

Kanban and Kaizen Defined and Compared

Kaizen is Japanese for "good change" – an improvement, a turn for the better. It is used for a philosophy of continuous development and continuous improvement. Kaizen is, if you like, a mindset, that involves the following ideas:

- that you achieve a lot by making little changes, one step at a time
- that you should always look to develop yourself and others
- that improvement has no limits; there's always room for more
- that every employee can help make change—from the shop floor up to the CEO
- that quality is important

- that the place to fix things is on the front line—on the factory floor, at the service counter, where the work is actually done
- that one of the best things you can do to improve is to get rid of waste (*muda*)

Kaizen is a Lean philosophy—everything you have read about waste in the Lean Six Sigma chapter stems from the Kaizen mindset.

It is also a philosophy that is opposed to the idea that change always comes from the top, that the boss knows best, the "command and control" mindset. It doesn't buy into the idea of the "hero entrepreneur" or the "great corporate leader". Kaizen says that every employee is responsible for improvement and that every employee can contribute hugely to the business. Napoleon, when he said, "every soldier of France has a marshal's baton in his knapsack," was actually making a very Kaizen statement!

You will sometimes hear the word *gemba* or *genba*, "the real place", which also means "the shop floor". It is a Kaizen idea that problems are actually visible—you just have to go to the shop floor, to the front lines, *out* of your office, and look for waste, defects, broken code or products or unhappy customers, and you'll see where the problems are and how to fix them. Again, this is very different from the idea that the "big boss" sits in his top-floor wood-paneled office behind his massive desk, and receives his top managers one by one to get their reports. It is about getting out there and getting your hands dirty.

Kaizen is a democratic mindset. Managers need to lead, but everyone's contribution is valuable. If you are leading a Kaizen project, make sure that you recognize every contribution. Give that trainee whose bright idea cut your defect rate in half, or the part-time cleaner who helped figure out where you could put the "buffer" stock that makes your system work faster, just as big a round of applause as the manager who reworked the process manual or the software engineer who sorted out the glitch in the order taking process. To get the best out of Kaizen, every single member of staff needs to feel they can speak out. And don't stop at full-time employees—contractors, too, have a huge amount they can contribute.

Kaizen is really easy to implement. You can start small, or you can start with a bang. Some organizations have had huge success with a Kaizen Blitz—targeting a specific area for just three to five days. One or two days will be spent training on Kaizen principles and philosophy, and the rest of the time on data collection, analysis, and implementation. A Kaizen Blitz uses the minimum expense and the maximum people to get what can be a terrific return. However, you should always remember that to get lasting results, you are going to want to follow up the Kaizen Blitz with a continuous commitment to Kaizen and with regular Kaizen projects.

Kanban is often found together with Kaizen, but where Kaizen is a philosophy, Kanban is a tool. It is "the card you can see", a way of visualizing work-flow.

Kanban comes from a Japanese factory floor practice. To ensure the orderly and speedy completion of work-flow, each order was given a card with the details of what product needed to be provided, and when. These cards were sent around the factory with the product as it made its way through the process. In each part of the plant, the cards representing these products were pinned to a board or hung on a frame. They were organized in three columns: backlog to do, work in progress, and "done".

As work was begun or completed, the card was moved from one column to the next. That way, everyone could see clearly what was in progress. Kanban improves the transparency of processes and projects that use it. And in line with Kaizen philosophy, information on the process is available to every shop floor worker or project team member—not just to the boss or project manager.

Once one product card went through to the "done" compartment, the worker would take another one from the backlog column, and start work on that. So, all day, workers were concentrating on one task at a time, and then moving on immediately to the next, with no time wasted.

Kanban is not just about visualization, and it is no longer limited to the factory floor, or indeed to manufacturing. Several key factors make kanban powerful:

1. Because the most important jobs in the backlog are placed at the top of the column, kanban prioritizes the tasks in the backlog. That's different from a to-do list, which doesn't usually show the different importance of the various tasks.

2. Because there's a limit on what can go in the "work in progress" column, kanban limits the amount of work being done and increases the focus on what's in progress.

3. Because every time a task is completed, another one is brought forward out of the backlog, kanban "pulls" work through the system. Team members don't have to wait for someone to give them a job to do—they can easily find one!

Kanban achieves in product manufacturing process environments the kind of things that Scrum achieves in programming and product development—focus, flow, and transparency. Like Scrum, it is effective and simple, but it manages multiple tasks at the same time, and while things don't change *within* a sprint in Scrum, with Kanban, you can quickly change priorities if the need arises. Kanban also works really well in a service environment; plenty of software developers also use kanban along with other approaches to help organize their time more effectively.

For many people, the biggest benefit of kanban it that reduces the kind of useless multitasking where nothing is ever finished because people are trying to do too many things and can't manage to complete any of them. It limits multitasking to what actually works—the limit is at the manager's discretion so that you can trim the limit to your environment.

The limit on the number of items in any column, and the prioritization of items in the backlog, also stop team members cherry-picking. For instance, in a programming team using kanban, if you only have two items that can be in code review at the same time, it stops team members saying, "Oh, I want to write new code. Can't someone else do the boring testing?" (Anyone who's ever worked in technology will know that problem!) And if every time a task is completed, a team member has to take one of the top two tasks from the backlog, they can't pick that easy job from halfway down.

Ways to Apply Kanban

The easiest way to get kanban working for you is really simple—you can just apply it to your work by putting up a kanban board in your office, or using an app like Trello or Smartsheet. You know what your to-do list is, so arrange it in the "to do" or "pending" column in order of priority. Some very small tasks can be high priority—for instance, paying the electricity bill!—while some quite large jobs can be lower priority, like getting three different insurance quotes for your renewal in two months. Select three of these tasks as those you want to get done now, and move them to the middle column—"in progress". Do them. When you have completed a task, move it to "done", and pull the next task off the "pending" column into the "in progress" column. Easy!

From there, it is a simple step to setting up kanban for a small team. There are just a few more things you need to do to implement it for a workgroup.

You will need to think about smart kanban policies. For instance, what conditions have to be met to post a task to backlog, or to move a task to "done"? What limits will you set on the number of stickies in a column? Does "done" mean before or after testing? You need to make sure that everyone is playing by the same rules; otherwise, it' is not going to work.

You might add extra columns. Some software teams add a "QA" or "testing" column so that work can be posted as finished subject to testing, moving it out of work in progress, and helping to pull more tasks forward from the backlog. Other teams use a "waiting for" column where, for instance, customer sign-offs are involved, or work depends on receiving third party components. It can also be useful to have a different color sticky for "blockers"—red is a favorite!

The key to making kanban work is:

- to minimize the "doing" column (minimizing work in progress creates focus and improves the work-flow)
- and to keep reviewing the board all the time—whether it's on everyone's desktop or up on the wall.

This magically encourages a state of flow in which tasks just jump out of backlog into "work in progress"—and the better the flow *is*, the better it *gets*. Kanban, at its best, is a virtuous spiral that keeps getting better.

Many people make lists, but lists can be overwhelming. They are often not well prioritized, and they show everything—the stuff you are actually working on, and the stuff you kind of ought to get around to but haven't started yet. Kanban makes life so much easier by focusing everyone on the stuff that is actually getting done. The rest is in the queue, but you are not fixated on it—its time will come!

Kanban and projects

Kanban can be tricky to apply across a project. If teams are delivering fast, sometimes the kanban gets so cluttered that you can't see the bigger picture anymore.

That is where a Kanban Portfolio Board can help. This holds the bigger chunks of work. These chunks are then broken down into smaller pieces, individual tasks, which can go on to a team board and be used to manage that particular team's output. So, as the project manager, you can visualize the project's progress on the portfolio board, but the teams can see their progress in detail on their boards.

Remember that kanban fits into the Kaizen philosophy, so it is about *continuous* improvement. It's meant to be a flexible process, so if you can see ways to improve the way you use it, don't hesitate to try them out.

You can use swimlanes on the project board, too. For instance, you might have one swimlane per product or one swimlane per client. You might have a swimlane for each team, or even for each team member. In much kanban software, you can collapse all but one swimlane, so project team members can see the whole project kanban board when they want to but spend most of the time focusing on their own kanban swimlane. That can help focus, particularly when you are managing one project with several teams (e.g., a process improvement project that's running across different factories or branches).

Once you get into kanban software, you can really deepen the way you use kanban. For instance, you can produce a cumulative flow diagram that shows how well you are doing turning your backlog into "done", and how fast you are doing it. WIP aging lets you see whether you are turning the whole of that middle column over, or whether there is some work in progress tasks that have hung around for ages and still not been finished.

You will be able to calculate your cycle time—how long it takes work items to get done. That is a key metric for continuous processes using kanban. Most project managers aim to improve their cycle time as the project team becomes more experienced.

Implementing Kaizen in Your Company

Some projects need a huge investment and make a big noise. Kaizen's not like that; it is not all-or-nothing, or an overnight change. Instead, it gradually builds change and achieves improvements over time, continually building on progress. It is gradual and incremental, and that means you can start small.

To work properly, Kaizen needs to be about habits, not just about process changes. You need to build it into your organization's DNA. You need to change the mindset. That is a challenge for the long term.

Still, you can get started quickly, even if it will take time to get Kaizen working at its full strength. The great thing about Kaizen is because of its emphasis on continuous improvement through small changes, it is eminently suited to small-scale implementation.

To get started, you will want to look for good opportunities for change. Be selective, and look for the "low hanging fruit"—problems that will be relatively easy to change but will make an appreciable difference to the quality, efficiency, or cost.

Where do you find problems? Finding problems is what Kaizen is all about! Once you have bedded Kaizen thinking into your organization, everyone will be finding opportunities for improvement all the time. And the best way to start is to involve everyone. Encourage teams to come up with ideas. Ideally, by the time you have finished, you will have created a workplace full of employees who not only don't resist change but also actively welcome and play their part in it. However, right now, you need to convince people to take that first step.

Whether you are just introducing Kaizen to your small team or playing your part in a company-wide implementation, you need to have enthusiasm and help others to feel the same way. It is great to brainstorm what you could improve, but be careful not to shoot people down if their suggestions are not quite what you had in mind.

It is particularly helpful to break down functional silos when you are introducing Kaizen. If marketing, sales, finance, and production all have a stake in a particular process, then you should aim to get all the people involved with the process to sit down together as a process improvement team. It may be the first time they have actually spoken to each other face to face!

Holding team meetings is a good way to get started. Explain Kaizen first, and then get started on finding those opportunities for improvement. Brainstorming is a great way to approach this. (If you're quite a forceful person, you might think about getting someone from the team to facilitate, rather than doing it yourself—that might help team members, particularly junior ones, feel confident to speak up.) Instead of asking for "problems we can solve", you could ask:

- what parts of the process are "sticky"?
- where do we have bottlenecks?
- what derails projects that you're working on?
- is there an approval or a stock item you always end up having to chase?
- what's your top "niggle"—silly little things that you just *know* are going to go wrong?

All suggestions should be written down—"the coffee machine breaks down too often" besides "cost of poor quality is 7.2% of product cost" and "finance approval for small orders takes too long." You can sort them out later. As, of course, getting the coffee machine working, while perhaps not top of the organization's list of priorities, is going to be a very popular improvement with your team, so it's one you might consider putting towards the top of the list!

Once the team has come up with a good list of problem situations, you can decide which ones you are going to tackle first. You might even get started on this in the same meeting. Now it is time to start working out how, using various techniques.

- 5Y's – asking "why, why, why?" until you get to the root cause. (The coffee machine breaks down because the nozzle gets clogged. Why? The nozzle gets clogged because it's not maintained. Why? It's not maintained because we chose a cheaper operator who doesn't do regular maintenance.)

- Brainstorming different solutions. Encourage creativity and innovative thinking – write down *every* suggestion even if it seems unlikely to help. Ask questions like "*What if* we did this?" or "*How* could we change that?" to get people thinking. Make sure once an idea's been put up on the board, you move along to other ideas—brainstorming has to keep moving, so you don't want to get stuck on discussing whether or not an idea will work.

After the brainstorming, take the ideas away and start working on them. It turns out the coffee machine is an easy fix; the contract comes up for renewal next month, and you have decided to switch back to the original supplier. Other problems need a bit more research put into them. For instance, changing the finance approvals on small orders will need a meeting with the finance team, where you might discuss why the approval is needed (for instance, to stop salespeople giving overlarge discounts) and what other ways you might address that need (for instance, a computer-based pricing model salespeople can use for pricing up those orders).

Implement as fast as you can, but on a small scale. Don't delay due to overthinking, second-guessing, or fear of taking risks—simply limit the size of the pilot. Build that pricing model and get one of your salespeople to take it out on the road with them. See how it works. If it works, roll it out across the sales force. If it doesn't work, you and the salesperson have wasted a few weeks, that's all!

In a large company, you almost need to think of your first implementation as "pirate", not "pilot"—it is taking a little piece of the business and making it a free pirate republic with a new process. It's not standardized. It's not in the job manual. If it works, *at that point,* you can roll it out across the company, and it becomes the new standard. But don't aim to make it the standard before you have tested it small scale.

Remember the New Coke debacle? If Coca-Cola had run New Coke just in California, or just in a selected number of stores, the message probably would have got back to headquarters that customers didn't like it. Instead, New Coke was rolled out across the entire US at one time. (Admittedly, the other big mistake Coca-Cola made was in not offering New Coke as an option, but retiring "old" Coke so that customers had no choice.)

Documentation is also very important, along with measurement. Just making improvements will only get you so far. You need to measure whether it is working. Put a sheet of paper on the wall by the coffee machine and ask people to note if the machine has broken down. (You *did* ask for an estimate of how often it was broken before, right? Or, if not, you *did* check how often it was breaking down before you switched operator, didn't you?) Check the figures for how many small orders are going through without needing approval, or for how quickly approvals are coming through.

"Where there is no standard there can be no Kaizen" is a common saying in the Kaizen world. So, while you might focus on pragmatic improvement, you also need to get the new processes written into job manuals and standards. The finance department needs to include the result of improvements in product costings and budgets. And you need to check that the results keep being delivered and that everything is on track. This is why Kaizen, though it empowers employees, also needs active managers. And it needs good data.

If you don't get the expected improvement, has a Kaizen project failed? No! Remember: Kaizen is about *continuous* improvement. So, if you haven't got the improvement, or you have only got a small improvement, then you need another iteration. You need to improve the improvement!

That is another reason why documentation is important. You have documented what you expected to achieve, and what you actually did achieve. Now you can look back and ask why you fell short. What did you *not* think of? What was the second-best idea, the one you didn't implement? Might that help now?

Documentation is often skipped, but there is another stage of Kaizen that's even more often left out. That is *reflection*, and it is a key part of becoming a learning organization. Sit down and think about the process of your first Kaizen project. How easy or difficult did team members find it to get the "feel" of Kaizen? Has it kept moving, or have people gone back to "business as usual"? What did you achieve? How do you feel about that—disappointed, ecstatic, somewhere in between? Where can you go next? Were there any difficulties getting buy-in from other departments in the business? Where can you go next?

This is not about data or hard benefits; it is about assessing the process and learning from your experience. Without this step, Kaizen is only skin deep. Include reflection as part of the process, and you are building Kaizen into the way you think about everything.

Personal Kaizen

This is the shortest section in this book. It is also, possibly, the single most important one.

You do not have to have an organization to apply Kaizen or apply it to business, either.

You can apply it to your cooking, your music-making, your investments, your life.

It is about learning and always wanting to do better. It's about reflecting on how you are doing and how you can improve.

Apply Kaizen to your life. You won't regret it.

Kanban With or Without Kaizen?

So: can you have Kaizen without kanban? Can you have Kanban without Kaizen?

Kanban is a tool and a very useful one. Kaizen is a philosophy or approach. So theoretically, yes, you could have one without the other.

However, you can use the kanban tool in other contexts. You can use it within Agile, for instance—it is a favorite tool for many Agile developers because it makes it so easy to visualize the tasks being completed. And even though Scrum and Kanban represent rather different views of how to organize tasks, some project managers successfully use "Scrumban" to blend the two. They take the fixed-length, time-boxed sprints and the project roles from Scrum, but the visualization, limits on work in progress, and focus on cycle time from kanban.

One great advantage of kanban for projects is that it allows *every* team member to see the state of *every* work item and its associated status. It is a very democratic tool compared to traditional project management methods, which only let the project manager see the whole project, and kept information highly controlled on a "need to know" basis.

But it has huge advantages. For instance, it could be a team member, not directly involved in a particular task or process, who, for whatever reason, spots the one thing that is blocking progress. A team member working on one aspect of a process may see someone else is working on something similar and ask for advice, or share a tip from what they have experienced so far. By allowing every team member to see the state of every work item, and associated status, you improve focus. Blockers are more easily identified, and dependencies can be seen better.

Kanban can also enhance focus, even within a sprint. Because only the "in progress" items are actually being worked on at any given time, the effort is concentrated on those items instead of being diluted among several different areas. That, together with the "pull" of the kanban process, can help make sprints faster and more efficient.

While a sprint delivers a single output at the end of the sprint, kanban is about continuous delivery—pushing software out as soon as it is ready, not waiting for the defined end of the sprint to do so. Its roots in Japanese manufacturing give it a focus on just-in-time value delivery that can be very powerful in accelerating cycle time—really good news for organizations that face a fast-moving competitive market.

Another way kanban differs from Scrum is that, in Scrum, the objectives are set in stone at the beginning of a sprint. In kanban, on the other hand, backlog items can be reprioritized very easily at any point in the process. That allows for fine-tuning *within* the sprint, just as sprints allow fine-tuning within the project. In other words, kanban can increase your agility—and your Agility!

However, while you can adopt kanban within another project management system, it is most often applied within a Kaizen environment, and it does work best when informed by Kaizen principles. For instance, it can incorporate Kaizen philosophy by having the process philosophies of Kaizen made explicit and integrated into your kanban system.

Kaizen can give team members better motivation. Because the mindset is about growth and improvement—personal growth as well as corporate improvement—, it is going to get the best out of your team. Because it is about continuous improvement in processes, it's going to keep improving your project. And it will help encourage the acceptance of new ideas—often a problem in organizations that have become set in their ways.

So, while you can use kanban without Kaizen, why would you?

Conclusion

Project management used to be a special subset of management. Most managers and entrepreneurs had very little to do with project management. They might have been asked to sit on a steering committee or free up one of their staff for a few days' project management, but that was it.

Today, though, project management is becoming a key management skill. Increasingly, line managers are responsible for running projects in their functional areas or across divisional boundaries.

Projects can often deliver a step-change in performance. They are a chance to stand back from "business as usual" and assess how well things are working—and then improve them. Launching a new product will almost always involve setting up a project; adding new capacity will often be done through a project rather than simply through the usual processes. If you work in an organization that has to deal with a fast pace of change in its markets or products—in software, for instance—, you will probably see many projects relating to new product development. So, learning how project management works and being able to use some of the key project management tools is crucial if you want to progress your career.

However, you might also consider moving into a career as a project manager. There may be opportunities for training within your organization; for instance, many businesses operate a training process for Lean Six Sigma. You could start out by taking Green Belt certification. If that suits you, and you do well on your first couple of projects, you might move on to Black Belt.

Project management is a skill that transfers well between businesses. There are always jobs in consulting firms for good project managers, where your experience of a given operating environment or industry will be an asset. So that is another way you could develop your career, if you wanted to. Some project managers even cut loose and start their own consultancies—and several of them have gone on to refine their project management methodologies. That is how Scrum was invented.

Running a startup or family business? Project management skills will help you improve your business—reduce your costs, launch new products, or simply improve your processes, so you don't spend all your time panicking and firefighting. If you are the kind of small business owner who regularly finds yourself working into the small hours to solve an issue or make sure an order goes out on time, or has to do the bookkeeping at weekends, project management and Kaizen might help you get your life back. Then you can be a business owner *and* a mom, or dad, or mountain climber, or home brewer… or whatever.

This book has taught you the basics of different project management methodologies and how you can apply them to your business. But if you want to go further, there is a "resources" chapter on the next page that can take you deeper into the subject.

Good luck with your projects!

Resources

There are plenty of good resources about—some free and some paid for. These include project management forums and software, as well as books that you can use to acquire a deeper understanding of a particular methodology.

Eric Ries' *The Lean Startup* is a useful guide for startups and smaller businesses. You don't have to know anything about Agile to get started with this book. It talks about Lean methodology, and it is highly business-orientated, unlike some books which get stuck more into the nuts and bolts of project management processes.

Coaching Agile Teams by Lyssa Adkins is a good book if you are struggling with introducing Agile to a more traditional management environment. It talks about how to create the right corporate culture for Agile teams and empower your project team members.

Mitch Lacey's *The Scrum Field Guide: Practical Advice for Your First Year* reviews basic practices and helps you get started managing Scrum meetings and sprint sessions. It is well rooted in real-world situations and includes information on managing contracts, which you will need if you have an external customer at the end of your project or process. Lacey warns, though, that although Scrum is very adaptable, you shouldn't cherry-pick your favorite bits—you have to commit yourself to Scrum in its entirety to get the best out of it.

Kenneth S Rubin's *Essential Scrum* is a key text for Scrum Masters, focusing on how the Scrum roles fit together and how sprints work. It is perhaps a little less user-friendly for the beginner than Lacey's book, but if you want to live the Scrum Master life, it ought to be on your bookshelf.

In the world of Lean Six Sigma, you could get *Lean Six Sigma for Dummies*—it is great for an entry point, though by the time you are thinking about black belt certification, you will probably have left it behind. It is very focused on Lean Six Sigma—you won't learn about other project management methodologies, but you'll be really well informed on Six Sigma by the time you're finished. A soberer approach to the subject, but equally good at explaining Six Sigma basics, is Greg Blue's *Six Sigma for Managers.* Greg is a Master Black Belt and a well-respected consultant, and the book is a clear and well-written explanation of what Six Sigma is and how it works.

For value stream mapping, the "Bible" is Karen Martin and Mike Osterling's *Value Stream Mapping: How to Visualize Work and Align Leadership for Organizational Transformation.* That is a long title, but the book itself is a very practical guide to the subject. If you are going to be doing extensive work in this area, it's really useful. Or you could consider John Shook and Mike Rother's *Learning to See: Value Stream Mapping to Add Value and Eliminate Muda*, which you can use as a workbook. However, it has a heavy focus on manufacturing—if you are in services, it may not be as useful.

Lean Analytics: Use data to Build a Better Startup Faster takes you through the subject in real detail. If you are lost in a fog of data and can't see which KPIs you need to look at right now, this book will help you. If you don't understand how some of the KPIs relate to your business strategy and priorities, it will help you with that, too. Anyone who lives in the land of click-throughs and conversions needs this book.

Robert Maurer's *One Small Step Can Change Your Life: The Kaizen Way* is a great resource for getting started with Kaizen. It is an inspirational guide to how you can bring Kaizen to your daily life. The same author's *The Spirit of Kaizen: Creating Lasting Excellence One Small Step at a Time* is also an introductory text but focuses on how to get Kaizen working in your organization. It is full of practical tips, real-world stories, and tools that are ready to use.

On the other hand, if you are ready to get into Kaizen in-depth, Shigeo Shingo's *Kaizen and the Art of Creative Thinking: The Scientific Thinking Mechanism* is your go-to tome. Shingo worked with Toyota and other major Japanese companies to improve their production processes, and the book is jam-packed full of useful stuff. If there is a key takeout, it's that you have to learn how to think outside the box—but that you can start to do so in quite a methodical way! It is a heavyweight book, but managers who have used it absolutely rave about it—it's the kind of book that you will go back to again and again.

If you work in software and want to implement kanban, you will love Arne Roock's *Stop Starting, Start Finishing*. It is an enjoyable, humorous read, but it is great for teams and managers that are new to kanban and focuses on how you can use kanban to limit work in progress and get more tasks actually done. You can also download a free ebook, the *Kanban Roadmap: How to Get Started in Five Easy Steps* from **https://info.planview.com/kanban-roadmap-_ebook_lad_en_reg.html**. Give a copy to every member of your team, and you have made a great start on the kanban journey.

Trello (trello.com) is a great software choice for managing kanban boards. It is a really simple app, but you can refine your kanban board by adding comments, attachments, or due dates to the cards. It's collaborative, so you can use it to link all your project members, whether within or outside your organization. And it runs on all kinds of Android and Apple devices so that you can easily keep a distributed project team in sync.

KaiNexus Software (kainexus.com) is also worth a look if you are headed the full Kaizen route. It has a fascinating and frequently updated blog, too, with reports from conferences, articles about new approaches, or about companies that are implementing Kaizen and Kaizen culture in general.

Projectmanagement.com is the Project Management Institute's web page, and it is one of the best places to see what's going on in project management, whatever particular flavor of PM you have adopted. There are plenty of articles covering a diverse range of subjects, from ethics to real-world case studies, specialized tools, and best practice tips for particular industries or tasks. PMTips.net is another great site with tons of listicles (like "5 ways to improve product testing"), career advice, how-to's ("Rescue and recovery of projects", which everyone will need someday!), and tips.

Part 2: Human Resource Management

The Ultimate Guide to HR for Managers, Organizations, Small Business Owners, or Anyone Else Wanting to Make the Most of Human Capital

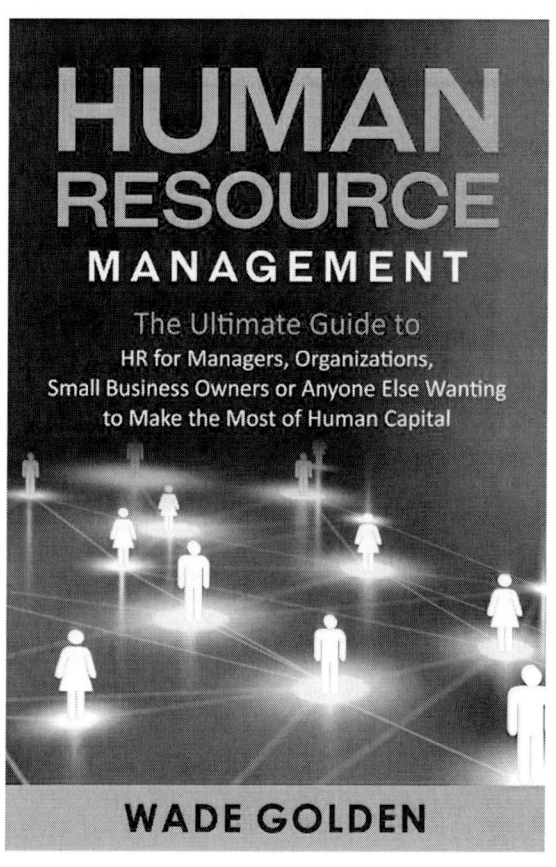

Introduction

Human resources are one of the best and most essential factors you must consider to grow your business. So, what are human resources? Human resources are the workforce in the business, comprised of people who lend their skills and expertise to help the business succeed. They determine the level of productivity, turnover rate and help companies achieve their goals in exchange for compensation.

Although other resources like capital, equipment, facilities, etc., are needed assets for any business's success, human resources are essential assets. They are the driving force of an organization. So, whether you produce goods or offer services, your business's success hinges on how you manage your workforce.

Because of the complex nature of people, human resource management requires skills and strategies. Your employees need motivation, satisfaction, and drive to make to keep them productive. Therefore, you must learn how to manage them so they do not become detrimental to you or your business.

It is vital to build core values around your business, so those onboard believe in the business vision, values, culture, and best practices that bring success. Recruitment, onboarding, and employee's performance analysis are strategies needed for effective human resource management.

Subsequently, it takes a well-rounded business owner or a Human Resource Manager (HRM) to effectively control and manage employees. You need human expertise to help you build a formidable team to ensure your business or company's progress. This book will equip business owners and HR managers with the best human resource management strategies to build a profitable business.

Chapter 1: What is Human Resource Management (HRM)?

Every organization thrives on its assets. These include the cash, equipment, facilities, infrastructure, and resources that generate revenue for the business. For example, a startup tech company needs data security, high-speed internet, and a landing page or website to thrive. But all of these will not be achievable if no one is willing to exchange his or her skills and abilities for compensation.

No company survives without its indispensable assets: its personnel. People make other assets in the company work. These are called human resources, and management of these resources is what you will learn in the first chapter.

What is HRM?

Human Resources Management or HRM is the management of the workforce within an organization by developing policies, strategies, and plans that enable the employees to work towards giving the business a competitive advantage. HRM permits the best workplace practices for employees through strategies that motivate people to work and achieve business goals and objectives. Also, it involves the approach a company takes to recruitment, training, compensation, and retaining its employees.

This kind of management is mainly two-fold: the personnel approach and the *employer-employees* approach. The former one concerns the old way of selection, recruiting, staffing, training, and payment of employees. This is an early version of human resource management and is primarily an administrative duty. But there is a need for a modern approach to HR management.

HRM can be viewed from a larger perspective than just the management-employee relationship. This approach is more concerned about factors responsible for employee performance and motivation to work and strives to enable a thriving workplace environment for employees within the organizational objectives.

The employer-employee approach makes HRM strategic by considering the complexity of humans. The way humans *think in the workplace* needs to be studied, and that's why there is an integration of psychology into HRM. Understanding how humans think, behave, and react is necessary for an effective HRM.

The knowledge about HR management equips you with all you need to direct and guide your employees to create a positive and conducive working environment. It allows you to manage workpeople-related issues ranging from recruitment to onboarding, training, performance assessment, payroll, promotion, etc.

For instance, in football, there are only eleven players in a team. Each team member plays in a position of strength for an optimal result, as directed by the coach. Now, a good coach must connect each team member's strengths to overshadow his or her weaknesses and strengthen the team to win the game.

Similarly, **HRM** equips employees with the necessary training and education on the job to help them work as a team for business success. Your employees might often need periodic on-the-job training, personnel analysis, and the right motivation to work.

Then there are two types of motivation: extrinsic and intrinsic. Extrinsic motivation is the external factors you employ just to motivate your employee to give their best on the job. This could be a pay raise, time-off, threat of job loss, and assurance vacation time or time needed for emergencies. Sometimes, this motivation might be positive; other times, it might be negative.

On the other hand, the intrinsic motivation for employees *is internally driven.* It stems from the employee with a personal desire to complete a task or overcome specific job challenges. So, **HRM** entails understanding the work scope and each employee differently before developing workplace policies that achieve better production and higher revenue.

In many organizations, a whole department is allocated for **HRM**. The **HRM** department is like the powerhouse of any business. It functions in both administrative and strategic affairs that concern the company. Regardless of how big or small your business is, you will require an **HRM** department. This makes your business well organized and coordinated.

Small business owners need an **HRM** because they also face personnel management issues. Problems among workers can have a decisive impact on business health. But management needs of a small organization are not of the same complexity or size as those of a large one. Still, these management issues also challenge smaller businesses.

Business owners who communicate personal expectations and company goals clearly, allowing employee feedback, have learned an essential human resource management strategy. Above all, human resources managers must develop empathy for their employees and get involved with them personally. This bridges the gap between top managers and subordinates while also maintaining a high level of professionalism to make sure that employees discharge their duties effectively. In this way, your business becomes more successful.

Historical Development of HRM

Human management is as old as humankind itself. Human resource management's earliest footprint is linked to how tribal chieftains were selected among the ancient civilizations. The practice involved safe and healthy strategies while hunting, which was then passed from generation to generation – until the Chinese introduced *employee screening techniques* in 1115BC. After that, the Greek and Babylonian civilizations developed "the apprentice system" before medieval times. All these systems recognize the need to train people for jobs.

HRM used to be personnel management because it involved more administrative roles than strategies. Employers that specialized in this were called the personnel managers (or personnel administrators). Then HRM evolved. It moved from the administration stage in the 19th century to the strategic human resource management of the early 1970s' in the 20th century.

The trade union took over early in the 19th century, changing theories of management. In the early 1900s, one of the foremost consultants, Frederick Winslow Taylor, brought about the logic of efficiency, proposing the theory of scientific management. This theory increases organizational levels of productivity through the greatest use of human labor.

Taylor observed that workers in many organizations seemed lazy. So, he suggested that one way to boost efficiency is to get the right person for the job, train the worker, and cause the individual to work maximally under strict supervision.

Also, Taylor encouraged a fair system of workers' compensation, which made his approach acceptable to both business owners and employees. Taylor's theory of management supported a balance between organization productivity and employees' remuneration. Workers were paid well for their work to make sure that the business increased in productivity. During these times, Human Resource Managers were simply *personnel managers* because of their administrative and supervisory roles.

The 20th century transitioned the **HRM** from supervision and administration to the professionalism of strategic human resource management (**SHRM**) and was responsible for the present-day Human Resources Management. HR professionals are more actively involved in business policies, work-life balance, and strategic planning that affect the company's growth.

The *behavioral science movement* came during the early 1960s. Douglas McGregor described two sets of assumptions about the nature of a person at work. He called it the theory "X" and theory "Y."

Theory X stands for the set of traditional beliefs that are negative, fixed, and inflexible. In contrast, Theory Y is positive, active, and flexible, with an emphasis on self-direction and integrating individual needs with organizational demands. This movement accepts the need to improve the quality of work-life to obtain increased motivation, which leads to improved results.

The works of various disciplines shape the history of human resource management. This includes managing the business, psychology, process management, information technology, statistical analysis, sociology, and anthropology. Also, the civil rights movement and legal cases were involved in the study of **HRM**, dealing with workers' rights and welfare.

Human resources management has evolved from a very primitive stage to now; changes in organizational structure are solely responsible for the evolution of HRM.

Why Human Resource Management?

In 2014, the average United States of America (USA) Company spent approximately $4,000 to fill a vacant position, which included the cost of recruitment and training for the employee. That was a lot of money, especially for small and medium scale businesses running on tight budgets. If a business hired the wrong person – who quit soon after being hired – that represented a significant loss.

Employees quit their jobs for several reasons. According to a West Monroe partner study in 2018, it was discovered that 59% of employees quit their jobs for a more appealing offer from other organizations. Another survey of 1,000 US employees by Dynamic Signal reports that two-thirds of the respondents considered quitting their jobs for lack of workplace communication. These and many other reasons (like unsatisfactory compensation, poor work-life balance, and job insecurity) were reasons employees quit despite the cost of hiring.

Now, how do companies hope to hire and retain their employees with all these inadequacies? What are cost-effective measures to ensure that the workforce improves? How would you avoid hiring and firing? All these can be avoided with proper management of human resources.

Human resources management gives you the skills, knowledge, and necessary tools needed to find and employ top talent. It also creates a good working environment for employees to succeed in their jobs.

HRM identifies the best recruitment strategy, selecting a talent sourcing approach, and works with onboarding new employees into the organization. HRM flanks a balance between you, your company, and the employees by enacting laws and policies with mutual benefits for all.

Another fundamental reason your business needs **HRM** is to help amplify productivity by boosting your employees' efficacy. HRM handles managing employees' many needs, ranging from financial to legal matters. Employees feel more like a part of a family when you show concern for their needs.

According to human resource expert Edward L Gubman, and author of the Talent Solution, HRM entails recruiting and retaining employees. He proposed that human resources' basic mission is to acquire, develop, and retain talent by aligning the workforce with the business. This enhances employees' contribution to the business.

The **HRM** designs an organizational framework that allows effective use of human resources and establishes a system that allows the business to function as one entity. This entails organization, utilization, and maintenance of the company's assets and its workforce.

Also, the **HRM** sees to the safety and health of the employees. Human resource management is directly related to health and safety for the workers in their working environment. You must make sure that your organization complies with federal laws that protect employees from hazards in the workplace. This projects a good image for your company and helps secure the future of such a business among other competitors.

Lately, organizations no longer run the business as usual. The face of businesses is changing gradually, and any company that wishes to rule the future must align with these changes. The 2020 COVID-19 pandemic ushered in a *new normal*, where many workers must carry out their duties from home. This new method of working is not alien to companies that had established policies for remote operation.

But many businesses are not used to having employees work remotely. They need to adjust to this new paradigm; they put their employees at high risk of being infected with the virus without doing so. While many businesses die off in times like this, others thrive and become even more productive. This is a risky time for many companies, but with the assistance of **HRM**, an effective risk management strategy peculiar to this time could be integrated into the organization's policies. This would protect not just the company interests and data, but that of the employee.

The new normal of the pandemic has become a great test for many company's **HRM**. **HRM** is more involved in virtual conference calling, email communication, and flexible work time with its workers. They know employees now work from home and are always with their families.

Whatever action the **HRM** department of any business takes at a time like this, it is sure to you spark reaction from the employees. Some workers might go to the extent of publicizing the company's name in an open forum like Reddit, Glassdoor, and another social media outlet. Employees will speak about their trust, fear, or support from the company. Poor **HRM** practices will automatically mean negative reviews from an employee who feels frustrated and wants to quit the job.

The owners or **HR** managers need to communicate the business values and philosophies with its workers adequately, or they will soon lose them. **HRM** has moved from merely solving personnel issues to contributing to the future directions and development of the organization and its employees. **HRM** handles both the performance enhancement of its employees and cost reduction strategies of the business, thus contributing directly to the productivity of the organization.

You need to flow with the tide of the time, or else your company risks going out of business. Your **HRM** department must learn to review the company's policies occasionally to allow it to fit with the looming technological advancement. For instance, in old times, job advertisements or vacancies were publicized in the newspapers. But in the present day, ads are placed on online job boards to enable professionals to find them.

Through the advancement of technology, globalization became an advantage rather than a threat to human resource management in the 21st century. You have to stay relevant and incorporate technology within HRM modules to achieve its purpose with a competitive advantage.

Functions of Human Resources Management

The HRM involves every facet of any company and is responsible for policy implementation, hiring, training, leadership, and usually controls the factors responsible for cash flow within any organization. HRM is the "people" arm of any business. The people are the workforce responsible for the organizational processes. HRM ensures that their needs are met. Typically, the HRM department runs the end-to-end management of the employee. They monitor the entry and exit plan of any employee within the organization. This department's major concern fixates on hiring and taking care of everything the employee needs until the individual quits or retires from the organization.

The old thinking of HRM was solely based on everything about hiring, training, appraisal, and payroll. But HRM had transited to be more strategic. It is preemptive and proactive in identifying tendencies of conflict and solves it before it happens. HRM controls the *people management* of any organizational process to keep to the organization's core values and work ethics.

Most successful companies today are those effective in leadership development among their employees through HRM, which instills company values and philosophies into the employees, making them feel like an integral part of the company. A sense of responsibility in your employees is developed by allowing them to perform on the job with little or no oversight from a supervisor and then rewarding them for excellent job performance. This is a business strategy that improves the employee's capacity to work.

HRM leadership development is both skill and organization culture development. You grow skills by practice while you develop the organizational culture through training and empowering workers to move up the chain.

Chapter 2: Basic Theories and Approaches of HRM

Human resource management theories, models, or approaches are principles coined from various disciplines necessary for human management. Most of these theories were principles in fields like psychology, philosophy, sociology, and the subject of natural science.

Many theories have been introduced into the HRM discipline. Sometimes, these are called *models* or *approaches*. The fact remains that whether you use a model or approach, understanding the basic principles for management in a clear and simple statement with a definite conclusion is what matters.

There are over 200 HRM theories developed by different management scholars. But we shall only consider the fundamental ones in this book and how you can apply them correctly to work for your business.

The Human Relations Theory of Management

In the early 20th century, Elton Mayo, an Australian-born psychologist and organizational theorist, began the Hawthorne study. He researched a group of people to look at human behavior and how this affects individuals in the workplace.

Taylorism – or the application of science in the workplace – was prominent during the times of Mayo's research. Taylorism is the scientific management of workers to improve productivity. Humans were seen as machines that could work under any condition, even when in unethical or unrealistic work environments. Mayo saw the need to replace the concept of "working machines" with social persons in the workplace. So, he popularized the idea of the social relationship at work, which means that employees should be treated as individuals with needs, not as machines.

The human relations theory of management postulates that people love to work and be a part of a team that enhances their growth and development. When employees realize the team spirit within your organization and see you are genuinely concerned about them, they would put in every effort to ensure productivity. The Human relation theory of management facilitates your business's economic growth through the support and motivation you give to your employees.

Everybody wants to feel they matter. In business, you need to show your workers you care for them and be interested in what matters to them. Doing this makes your employees feel part of something that works. So, they will give their best to produce high-quality products or services.

For instance, TGIF management (Thank Goodness It's Friday), an American restaurant, flew 400 of its employees to a party in Florida in 2013. Although that might seem costly and could affect the company's profitability, the action reflects the company's concern for their employees. Acts like this eventually motivate employees to work better and harder.

Therefore, the human relation approach to work requires that business owners or managers possess special kinds of skills. While you must have leadership skills as a business manager, you need to manage other skills to manage both your business and your employees: *human relations skills*. There are five (5) of these skills in the workplace.

1. Communication Skills

Effective communication is essential to workplace ethics and success in business. You must understand how you communicate well with your employee in such a way that it boosts their morale, affects their performance, and increases productivity. A business owner who seeks to learn the human relationship management well must know how to say what matters and engage the employees in decisions, choices, and the company's change in policies.

Always be in constant touch with your employees. Pass down memos. Discuss the company's vision, goals, and objectives with your employees. Learn to reiterate the company's value to them. Ask questions and listen to your employees. Give instructions. Look at their body language and facial expression while you are with them. A lot of what we communicate is non-verbal.

Your ability to communicate is not only in words. You need to understand non-verbal gestures and understand unspoken signals. Those things not only make you an effective communicator but also allow you to know if you are on the same page with your employees – or not.

2. Conflict Resolution Skills

Due to employees' personality differences, it becomes difficult to avoid conflict as these differences make us see the world from different perspectives. Conflict can infuse strong emotional reactions between coworkers, and this does affect the company's level of productivity. You must develop effective conflict resolution skills so strife among your workers will not liquidate the business. Managing individuals with different personality types and worldviews can be a difficult task, but not an impossible one.

One key to conflict resolution is your ability to identify conflict before it starts. When you notice feelings of resentment among your employees, you need not wait until it aggravates. Take the time to help your workers interact as a team, discussing any resentment you notice. One-on-one interaction with your employees helps guide against conflict.

Also, learn to watch out for possible causes of conflict among employees. There would never be conflict without reason. Issues of poor job quality, sudden request for a change in a team member or projects, and behavioral shifts are indications of conflict.

You need emotional intelligence to resolve any conflict in your organization. Although you cannot make everyone on your team happy, you can work to recognize an emotional lag amidst your workers and fix it. It is okay when your employees disagree on a matter, but you must learn to bring them to a consensus by making them see different things from the same perspective.

3. Multitasking

Multitasking is the ability to manage many tasks without getting out of balance. It involves switching back and forth between tasks. For example, responding to incoming mails while instructing your employees reflects multitasking skills. Your business success depends on how best you can manage your time and tasks well.

Managers have a lot of tasks, questions, and issues to solve daily. They manage their own schedules while managing others to make the most effective use of their time to increase productivity. Aside from your many primary responsibilities as a manager, your employees are your responsibility

You don't want to feel stressed-out while multitasking; eventually, you might overreact with your employees. High emotions (due to stress or fatigue) can be detrimental for a manager. Here are a few ways you can improve your multitasking skills without damaging your managerial stance:

- Create a to-do-list

Your to-do list should contain your work plans for the day. Schedule it the night before to avoid putting yourself under too much pressure.

- Make time for prioritized tasks

Identify your tasks by differentiating between urgent (must-do immediately) and the simpler-yet-important tasks awaiting completion. First, complete the most urgent, important tasks. Then address the less-urgent ones.

- Monitor your progress

Your to-do list will help you monitor what has been done and what is yet to be done. Discover if you are behind schedule and make the adjustment.

- Avoid distraction

Distraction reduces your ability to focus on your job. Keep distractions away and learn to concentrate on the task at hand. This may require you turning off your gadgets and going to a quiet area to work.

- Delegate duties

Your ability to delegate will help both you and your employees to work as a team. Check your not-so-important tasks and delegate them to your employees. For example, you might have to visit a client for a presentation and make a social media post for your business. Ask the digital marketing team to take care of the social media post while you visit your client.

4. Negotiation Skills

Negotiation happens regularly in business. Managers negotiate when trading, recruiting, and trying to reach an agreement with a client. You need strong negotiation skills to meet your employees' needs, as there will be time spent discussing pay and performance. This might not go well without good negotiation skills.

Managers must be objective in terms of their skills, keeping in mind the possible response of the other party in a negotiation. You should be careful not to allow outbursts of emotions to muddle your choice of words. Also, avoid confrontations.

Don't ever let employee negotiations go public. If it does, the media has its way of making the situation look bigger – and worse – than it is. For example, media scrutinized Unilever's industrial face-off over unpaid pension, creating a controversy that was blown out of proportion and was not professionally managed.

5. Organization Skills

Being organized is an essential skill for business owners and HR managers, especially when the business is growing and expanding. The growth of any organization implies more tasks, more clients, and a need to increase the workforce. The organization's skill entails your ability to control your business growth, workspace, and coordinate workflow within your organization.

Organization skill helps business owners manage their time and guarantee efficiency in every task. For example, a highly organized way of sending bulk emails, filing paperwork, and keeping your desk tidy saves you a lot of time and energy.

Human Relations Management Theories

Human relations management theories are principles used by business owners and managers to manage their human resources' capacity and productivity. These theories serve as a guide on how to relate with your employee in the workplace. The purpose is to enhance efficiency without a clash of interests.

One of the foremost management theorists, Elton Mayo, proposed that human relationship is the most critical factor that affects productivity in the workplace (Mayo's Hawthorne studies). Mayo observed that workers become more efficient in their jobs when they work together as a team and support one another to achieve the organization's goal.

Additionally, Mayo saw that workers feel more motivated to work when attention and recognition are provided. This produces the Hawthorne effect.

Abraham Maslow's Motivational Theory

The Abraham Maslow Motivational theory, sometimes called the theory of need, creates a new model for human relations management. This theory focuses on employees' needs, rather than what the employees can do for the company.

Maslow's assumption was that managers should consider their employees' needs, starting from the bottom to the top of the pyramid. Understand that your employees have needs that must be fulfilled in the workplace.

How Maslow's Theory Fits with Human Relations in Management

After the Hawthorne studies, Abraham Maslow's theory showed the direct correlation between human needs and their motivation to work. Maslow's five basic needs (physiological, safety, love, esteem, and self-actualization) are the motivating factors that make up an employee's work values.

The first instinct for any human is survival. This is the lowest level of basic human need. An employee will find it difficult to work if that basic need isn't available. These basic needs include salary and job stability. Also, employees want to feel secure, such as working in a safe and hazard-free environment. Once the first basic need is accomplished, the next thing that employees want is a sense of belonging and cooperation with other co-workers. Correspondingly, a desire for respect and a positive self-image follow. Finally, there is the top of the pyramid—self-actualization. The ultimate need for any employee is autonomy at work, coupled with the feeling of excitement about their achievements in the workplace.

A real-life application of Maslow's theory in the business world is how Wegmans supermarket treats their employees. Of course, your first choice of jobs might not be working in a supermarket due to its low pay and lack of job security. However, that is not the case for a company like Wegmans, considering they provide their workers with a 100 percent medical insurance premium (an example of *psychological needs*). Also, Wegmans hires workers in their early teens, and most Wegmans managers started working there in their teens (an example *of security needs*). Plus, this grocery store occasionally provides its managers with a company-sponsored trip (touching on *self-actualization needs*).

You can clearly see how Maslow's theory intertwines with the business structure of the Wegmans supermarket. This company remains one of the leading grocery stores in America, with an annual sale of over $9.7 billion, for a reason. The company satisfies their workers' needs, and in turn, these employees gladly honor their commitment to work. Subsequently, this creates an increase in sales and revenue.

It's important to recognize that employees' needs change with time. This is why human relations are essential in assessing and managing the changes in human needs. Otherwise, the purpose of this approach in business would be lost. Flexibility is required when dealing with different people because no two employees are the same. What works for one might not work for the other. Although Maslow's theory can help resolve human needs in the workplace, it is not the one and only general rule to management theory.

Other diverse human relation management theories are employee focused. Below are four (4) basic human relation theories that will help you value your employees, which will cause a subsequent increase in your level of productivity.

- Organization life cycle theory
- Resource dependency theory
- Strategic contingency theory
- Organizational learning theory

Organization Life Cycle Theory

The organizational life cycle is the life cycle of a business, from its creation to its termination. It refers to the expected sequence of advancements that any business experiences, including inception, growth, maturity, and eventually, its death. This sequence of events depends mainly on the nature of the company's workforce.

Five Stages of the Organization's Life Cycle

- Stage One (Existence): I call this the *birth stage*. It signifies the concept of the business, which involves acquiring customers and creating strategies to retain them.

- Stage Two (Survival): At this stage, businesses seek to grow and improve their capacity, setting goals and objectives to generate more revenue. Hence, the reason they try to develop employees' skills or increase the workforce.

- Stage Three (Maturity): At this stage, your organization enters a proper hierarchy of management. No organization can survive beyond this stage without the correct structure that properly supports teamwork, creativity, and innovation among workers. Businesses seek to outlast competitors in this stage with high-performance through its human resources.

- Stage Four (Renewal): The stage of renewal focuses on reviving the business's value while also exploring new possibilities. You must make more informed and analytical risk at this stage of the life cycle. This is where you encourage flexibility and innovation among your employees by allowing them to bring new ideas to the table for discussion.

- Stage Five (Decline): Well, all good things must end. This stage initiates the death of the business. Several factors contribute to a business dying. These include an adverse external environment, a decrease in competitive advantage, a political agenda, and employees placing importance on personalized goals over the company's goals.

But the decline stage does not necessarily mean the organization is on its last leg. It could bring about independence, diversification, or even the successful revival of the business.

Resource Dependency Theory

This is basically the study of how the external resources of organizations affect the behavior of the business. It was one challenge managers faced during the economic recession in the 1970s.

The resource dependency theory relates to how best your organization acquires scarce resources, including human labor, and uses them for competitive advantage in the market.

Consider the case study of ALDI, a leading retail store in Europe. This company enacts a policy that makes their employees internal stakeholders within the company. Because employees feel part of the organization, they give their best on the job. This is an HR-centric strategy that produces an excellent competitive advantage for ALDI.

Strategic Contingency Theory

The strategic contingency theory strategy helps businesses thrive within a complex, competitive environment by developing highly profitable strategies with the least amount of risk. These strategies can contain both dependent and independent variables.

For instance, when Cheapo Toys, a corporation that sells toys, experienced a setback, they tried to improve their organization by studying the different variables that affected their employees. Cheapo Toys wanted to understand what had affected worker productivity, turnover, absenteeism, and job satisfaction.

Motivation and leadership are just two examples of the many independent variables of the contingency theory. At the same time, productivity, turnover, and absenteeism are examples of Dependent variables. Their conclusion was to overhaul the company's strategy by improving workers' job satisfaction.

As a business owner, you will need to think outside the box. You can use trial and error to ascertain what variables provide the required results for your business in times of crisis.

Organizational Learning Theory

The organizational learning theory is the ability of an organization to adapt to changes that would make them relevant and effective, even in the future. This theory proposed that knowledge is the hallmark of a successful business that would rule the future. It involves learning new trends, technologies, and ways to survive the evolution in business.

Most organizations cannot compete favorably with today's advancements simply because they become too rigid to flow with the world's changes. Any organization that does not embrace learning will soon fizzle out because of fierce competition. Learning is an advantage for business survival, and based on the organizational learning theory, you must build a learning culture into your business to guarantee its success.

The "Soft" and "Hard" Approaches to Human Resource Management

Basically, there are two broad approaches to managing, developing, motivating, and coordinating any business's human resources. The approach you use is extremely important to the wellbeing of the business.

The Hard Approach to HRM

The "hard" approach treats employees as just another resource within the organization. Seeing human resources the same way as other assets like the machinery, infrastructure, and cash flow. The key factor in this HRM approach is to get the best of all resources, including human resources, in terms of increased productivity.

Managers use this approach to maximize profit and minimize cost. This approach's key features include lack of job security, little or no communication from leaders and managers, judgmental job appraisal (good or bad), and offering employees little autonomy of work.

The Soft Approach to HRM

This says that employees aren't just like any other resource. It views employees as the most crucial business resource and a potential advantage over the competition. The "soft" approach asks how they can obtain the right skills for the business. It seeks to know how to train, develop, and motivate employees to give your business a competitive advantage in the market.

This approach treats employees as individual entities who have needs and who require motivation to work. Employees enjoy the autonomy of work and enhanced long-term work plans for both the business and its workforce.

The question now is whether to use the soft or the hard approach for your business. Well, no *one* system is right or wrong.

It all depends on what you plan to achieve in your business. In fact, you can merge various aspects of the two approaches as you wish.

Right now, the soft approach seems most prominent in the business world because it values and respects employees, rather than treating them as if they were machines. Since the soft approach requires training and development, it implies that it is not cost-effective. But you might get your return on investment after up-skilling your workers.

A major disadvantage of the soft approach is that it creates a delay in decision-making, unlike the hard approach. You do not need a consultation with your employees to make decisions using the hard approach. It gives the autonomy of the business to the owner.

So, either you choose the soft approach, hard approach, or integrating the two; the decision is up to you. Your choice of approach depends on what you plan to accomplish. Business owners must learn to find what uniquely works best for their business. If at any point, a management theory seems unfit for your business, you can change it and apply what does fit.

Chapter 3: The HR Manager and Other Key Roles

What are your key roles in business as a human resource manager? Many people now know the importance of HRM within any organization, so this chapter will consider an HR manager's roles and duties. You will gain appreciation for the HR role with the employees and the organization.

Generally, an HR manager is a pass-to man or woman for all worker-associated problems. Your duties involve dealing with activities like recruitment, talent sourcing, performance control, and training of employees. Human Resources is an essential part of any business, which is why every business needs an HR department with a manager to manage, motivate, and coordinate human resources.

An organization's capacity to grow and develop is primarily based on the attitude of its employees. The employees represent the intellectual capital, which can either make or destroy a firm's efforts to stay relevant in the market.

Finding and maintaining top talent can be difficult. You need to sort through many applicants to find a specific candidate that the company needs for your vacant position. This implies that the power to choose the business's workforce rests on the HR manager, so care must be taken to avoid mistakes that could cause a significant business loss.

This chapter aims to reveal the HR manager's detailed roles and how he or she can effectively carry out these duties within the organization. Also, you will learn how to promote company values and shape the lives of its employees. HR managers should be people-oriented and result-driven, with exceptional skills in terms of human resources management and knowledge about HR best practices of the 21st century.

Roles of a Human Resource Manager

There are six simplified roles of the HR manager, broken down for this book to cover these responsibilities:

- Development and implementation of strategies that align with the overall business strategy
- The go-between for management and the employees
- Coordinates the recruitment, selection, and onboarding of new employees
- Supports current and future business needs through developing human capital
- Develops and monitors the overall HR strategies and company policies across the organization
- Creates a conducive working environment
- Oversees and monitors employee appraisal to drive high performance
- Responsible for employees' compensation, remuneration, and other workplace benefits
- Ensures legal compliance throughout human resource management

1. Participate in Strategic Planning

HR managers are brilliant planners. They determine the company's long-term goals and use the available resources to achieve them. Strategic planning involves developing a model for the business that will help it survive. The HR strategy must align with the business strategy and give it a competitive edge in the market.

Different companies may have different goals. Those within the same industry will not likely have the same goal. This is because a company's goal is based on the specific needs of the organization. For example, companies selling digital software will provide a hassle-free use of their services. Retail-marketing agencies will strive to increase customer loyalty. So, the HR manager has to understand the company's needs and then apply strategies that meet that specific need.

So, how can you identify the company's specific needs as an HR manager? What human resources techniques would you apply? How would you implement your strategic plans? Let's look into the stepwise order of an HR strategic plan.

Step 1: Evaluate the Current Business Situation

Your strategic approach begins with a plan. You cannot effectively plan without first knowing the current situation of the business. Now, how then can you evaluate the business situation?

- Assess current HR capacity: Catalog the human resources available. Identify your employees' skills, degrees, and work experience. This will help you understand your workforce capacity and how they can help the business fulfill its objectives.

- Evaluate HR data: This analyzes the business turnover rates, the causes, and future workforce gaps. It forecasts the HR needs in terms of demand for more employees, training of current employees, and identifying skills needed for vacant positions.

- Conduct a SWOT analysis: SWOT in business is a short form for strengths, weaknesses, opportunities, and threats. The first two relate to the company internally. They are the company's capabilities and limitations, respectively. Because these factors are internal, they are within your control. Examples of these include business reputation, location, and the workforce.

But the last two in the analysis are opportunities and threats, which are external factors that affect the business market. It includes market prices, supplies, and competitors. Although you cannot change them, you can take advantage of them as opportunities or protect yourself from them (threats). HR managers can engage in a brainstorming session to know which four factor the company needs to consider most when planning.

Step 2: Estimate Future HR Requirements

The success of a business is based on working towards specific goals and objectives. Anything short of these puts the company at risk of significant loss. Thankfully, HR managers make sure that companies achieve these goals. They lay the groundwork for the company to meet a certain standard and any future demands in terms of market analysis, budget analysis, staff management, prediction of market curve, and productivity.

How Do You Estimate the Future HR Requirement?

- Reviewing the company's vision and mission statement: A statement comprised of a company's vision and mission that highlights set goals that the company aims to achieve within a stipulated time. They hold the beliefs and values of the company. The HR managers must periodically follow up on how they work towards achieving these vision and mission statements.

- The use of supply and demand: This determines slack in the company's human resources' sector. There is a need to balance the company's workforce capacity by estimating the number of workers needed to prevent a shortage or an excess of workers.

Step 3: Develop Strategic HR Objectives

HR managers take strategic steps to make sure other company divisions contribute to achieving the business's vision and mission.

This is known as the *Strategic HR Objectives*. It requires the HR manager to work hand in hand with other departments within the company to achieve the stated goals.

For example, to accomplish the company's sales objectives, the HR department may have to work with the sales manager to develop an effective and competitive incentive plan for the company's sales representatives.

How to Develop Strategic HR Objectives

- Devise an effective plan to achieve your objectives: Each objective consists of a specific set of steps. For instance, the business contingency of a company may involve cross-training workers so business activities remain uninterrupted in cases of emergencies.

- Plan for contingencies: Businesses may decide to take an unplanned turn. The HR manager will need to devise a plan that will compensate for these unexpected cases.

- Track your success analytics: This is a way to know how close you are to your target objectives. This is where the metrics measurement of performance comes into play. This involves data representation of an organization's strength, success, abilities, and overall quality. The HR metrics chosen should match with the strategic objectives of the company.

Step 4: Monitor and Evaluate

After the strategic HR plan has been designed and set in motion for a period, you must measure your progress. This will allow you to know if you need to intensify your efforts or re-strategize.

How to Monitor and Evaluate Your Progress

- Conduct Reviews: To track your progress, conduct a yearly or a 6-month review, depending on which one fits your business. This involves an assessment of your employees and other staff. Try to use the workforce metrics you've selected in the previous step.

- Determine the factors affecting your strategy: These factors may be internal, i.e., within the company. Sometimes, it could be external too—for instance, the launch of a product similar to yours by a competing organization.

The human component is inevitable in achieving the company's objectives, except for several tools and software, depending on availability, which automate the process. These tools are useless without a highly motivated and skillful employee to operate and manage them. The quality of your HR processes and your staff are a strong determining factor of how your company's objectives are realized.

2. Provide Quality Career Development Assistance

Today, businesses succeed due to the developmental programs provided to the employees. Because of this, HR managers seek to retain workers through professional improvement, competency mapping, overall performance management, education, and mentorship, to get the most efficiency.

Career development refers to programs designed to shape a desired character, talents, and profession with modern-day and future opportunities within the company. Since it focuses on future prospects, it has a protracted-term orientation and is needed to develop career plans. This development helps employees meet their career aspirations and equips them for the job required within the organization.

As an HR manager or business owner, you must mandate employees to strive for self-development to prepare them for the business's future. The career development model shows that organizational and individual career planning should be integrated into the business's developmental strategies.

Career development is crucial for the implementation of a professional plan. This sets the direction for a worker to improve and move up the ladder in their career. The principle goal of professional improvement is to ensure that people with suitable qualifications and reviews are available while needed.

Professional development is a critical issue of career control, emphasizing advancing employees' careers, and increasing business efficiency. This development should commensurate with the requirements of the organization.

HR managers should conduct a check on employees once a year to review their performance. This includes a reward for good performance or a rebuke for failing to fulfill set goals. The employees are also considered for promotion, demotion, re-association, and replacement within the company. A few creative HR managers roll out career plans, techniques, and improvement plans for their employees to sustain their motivation.

As a result, the HR supervisor should spend effort and time to layout and broaden career plans that would be an addition for both the employees and the business. Employees' career development has proven that such a mindset helps them produce quality outcomes.

3. Advocate for Employees Through Labor Laws

Some argue that the HR manager is there solely to defend the business. If so, what happens when the matters about employees' rights arise? Who defends employees when they are being cheated? Who represents them in the boardroom when decisions that would affect the workforce are being made? Of course, the HR manager has a duty of advocacy to the employees too.

The HR managers enact policies and guidelines that allow employees to engage actively with the management in matters that concern them and their welfare. Strong advocacy encourages workers to carry out their duties efficiently and help the company fulfill its goals and objectives.

Also, HR managers can help balance his or her responsibilities to the employee and employers by creating advocacy programs. This program can include guidelines for employees' use of social media, health and safety measures by the management, and guidelines on workplace behaviors.

4. Ensure a Well-Structured Reward System

Human Resources experts do not conduct payment analysis on their own. They allow the company's board of directors to perform this task to verify its protection. This is usually done under attorney-client privilege. HR experts also do not provide legal advice about compensation fairness, but their roles revolve around administration, compensation, incentives and reward systems, and structural and differential payment.

Let's consider a few of the roles of the HR manager in guaranteeing fair compensation among employees.

- Make the right offer

When a person is newly employed, he or she is accurately placed within the already existing salary scale relative to the internal equity. If the employee negotiates, an agreement is reached, documented, and then preserved.

The HR manager must consider various factors like education, labor skills, work experience, and other factors while making the right offer for the new hire. The Human Resources Manager needs to make sure that the pay grade fits the skilled job in question.

- Monitor Merit Increases

As an HR manager, you decide what behavior or attitude makes an employee deserve a promotion or an upward pay scale after close observation of performance. Before the merit increase of an employee, the HR manager must adequately and fairly rate their performance. This can be accomplished by evaluating the overall ratings of the employee's performance. They also must question decisions that are not merit-based and stop any recommendation for merit, which negates laid down policies.

- Consider a Pay Audit

When conducting pay analyses, the HR manager should follow the counsel's legal advice and keep the information confidential. You can take the lead by pointing out when a pay audit is needed. As the manager, make sure top leadership is prepared to take corrective action as required before that investigation is underway.

It is expected that differences in pay will be brought to the forefront and addressed during auditing. If these things are not well addressed, it could be considered illegitimate and be regarded as theft. So, in conducting a pay analysis, you must make sure that the differences in pay among employees performing similar jobs can be accounted for. The payment analysis identifies all employees who fall below and above the minimum and maximum pay range and respectively account for this pay inequality.

- Job Grouping with Care

Neglecting to present all equivalent job titles the same way is one mistake human resources managers often make. A lot of employers allow job titles to be in an open forum. For instance, an employee is described as "a Human Resources Manager," while another is called "HRMGR resources. Notably, spreadsheet software, such as Excel, Open Office, or Lotus 1-2-3, will not recognize the title as the same.

5. Contribute to a Great Working Environment Through Good Employment Relations

Another HR manager's role is to deliver a good working environment for the employees through a mutual relationship. As a Human Resources manager, you are expected to create and maintain a good relationship with your employees. This involves keeping tabs on them and their wellbeing.

A good relationship keeps employees loyal and motivated to do their jobs. In most organizations, the human resources department is responsible for this job, but other organizations have an employee relation manager for this specific role.

The Employee Relation Manager bridges the gap between an employer and an employee, resolves workplace issues, and comes up with programs and policies that aim to employee overall satisfaction. These policies may include accurate compensation, paid leave, reasonable working hours, and other programs of benefit to the employee.

Maintaining a good relationship with your employees requires you to view your employees as stakeholders of the company, rather than just mere paid workers that can easily be replaced. This perspective makes the opinion of the employee valid and valuable, which can be of great benefit to the company. An organization that has the best interest of its employees at heart will always succeed. This is because they have the best interest of their workforce at heart. The employees then increase the productivity level.

The HR manager handles workplace issues, and including problems between employees and employer and employee complaints about working conditions. The HR manager also attends to the complaints of unfair employment practices, office politics, discrimination, diversity, and a lot more. The employee relations sector of HR must be capable of handling all these workplace issues.

The most important duty of the HR manager to the employees is guaranteeing job satisfaction. HR evaluates how satisfied an employee is while working in an organization. You should be concerned with whether an employee enjoys working in your company or not. Evaluate your employees' morale and conduct a periodic survey among them to know how they feel about their jobs.

6. Performance Management

Employee performance is based on the relationship between the employee and the employer, and a good employer-employee relationship is crucial in the development and implementation of performance management systems. The HR manager monitors any issue related to the employee's job performance. Beyond performance appraisal, HR managers now actively participate in the day-to-day running of the business.

Performance management is a process where the HR manager evaluates the progress of employees according to their performance. Sometimes, certain situations might change the course of the job. The HR manager has to communicate these changes and make sure workers are flexible to adapt to the new changes.

Most times, performance management is not just about rewards and evaluation. It also involves planning with your employees, executing your plans, and analyzing the result afterward. This helps you align the company's goal with your employees' work. By working with your employees, you can boost their commitment to work, which leads to an increase in productivity.

Performance management is essential because it allows HR managers to get feedback from their employees. You do not know how much your workers love or hate their job until you give them a chance to openly communicate their opinions. This is a feedback strategy for performance. Also, HR managers should learn to recognize employees' effort on the job and appraise good work.

Chapter 4: Onboarding and Recruiting Tactics

How do you find the best applicant for a job as an HR manager? What do you consider in your selection of the right candidate during recruitment? What is the most effective strategy for recruitment? These questions – and many more – are significant concerns for managers in recruiting and onboarding candidates for vacant positions.

According to a Harris Poll survey of 225 human resource managers and 2,027 employers, 48 percent of the respondents acknowledged that finding qualified candidates to fill positions is a top concern for them. This indicates that over two-thirds of human resource managers are worried about onboarding the right candidate to fill a vacant position.

The good news is you do not have to worry anymore. This chapter will help you identify, select, and onboard the right candidate for your business or organization's specific vacant position.

Why Onboarding and Recruitment Matters

The term "onboarding" is frequently used to describe the process of bringing new workers on board in a new workplace. This process requires a lot of documentation, orientation, and helping the new staff acclimate themselves with the work environment on the first day and beyond.

Usually, onboarding takes a day or a few weeks. Sometimes, the length might be extended until the employee has completed their first year of work, depending on the organization's culture and workplace practices, but onboarding differs greatly from recruitment—you onboard staff after you have completed the recruitment process.

Recruitment entails finding the right candidate out of a vast population of job seekers for a vacant position. Martins Luenendonk, an economist and a capitalist, defines recruitment as finding and hiring the best and most qualified candidate for a job opening in a timely and cost-effective manner.

The recruitment process is essential to increasing the human resources within your organization, either for expansion or to grow the company's annual revenue. But it is not enough for business owners or managers to increase their profit margin by recruiting more human resources. More so, you need to find the specific person that fits the vacant position within the company. Then equip the person with the required skills to carry out their duties in the new workplace.

So, it does not end with recruitment; you need to hire the required skill and then train the person to suit your company's work practices. So, onboarding is as important as the recruitment process because these two processes contribute largely to the growth and development of the business or organization.

Since recruitment process precedes onboarding, below are the five (5) significant recruitment guides you must follow:

- Recruitment Planning
- Talent Sourcing
- Screening of Applicants
- The Job Offer
- Induction of the New Employee
- Onboarding

Recruitment Planning

The best way to start any worthwhile process is to plan for it. You build a house by first getting the architectural plans on paper. The plan is the infrastructural design of your proposed building on paper. It serves as the guide for all your building actions afterward. Similarly, as a business owner or an HR manager, you must understand that the first step for a recruitment exercise is planning.

A recruitment plan saves you the energy you would have spent on an inadequate recruitment exercise. This is the first and the most critical recruitment stage, considering the whole process rests on the plan. An effective strategy helps you save your time, energy, and the possibility of short-handing your workers.

Every organization needs the right team to function optimally but taking on a bad egg as a team member can be detrimental to the organization. Hence, the need for strategic recruitment plans.

There are four key elements you need to put into consideration in your recruitment plans. These are:

Job Analysis - The job analysis involves identifying and describing the vacant positions in your organization. This can be completed by checking out the skill gap within the organization and determining how this lag affects your company's productivity.

The job analysis can be done by identifying your business's turnover rate, the department that needs more workforce, and why. A study like this helps you recognize the vacant position and discover why you need to hire a new candidate for it.

Job Specifications- The next one is the job specification. You not only identify the expertise needed for the vacant position, but you also consider other factors like experience, knowledge, emotional intelligence, qualifications, personal qualities, and attributes that best fit the job.

Job Description-This provides you with information about the scope of the job. It describes the responsibilities and positioning of the job within the organization, and it helps you know what prospective candidates must possess to meet the demands of the job.

Here is a checklist to help you in your job description:

- Organization name and description
- Organization core values
- Benefits offered by the organization
- Job location
- Job summary
- Job requirements
- Job title or Job identification
- Description of duties and responsibilities
- Working condition
- Compensation and benefits

Therefore, you must review your job description periodically in your recruitment plan. This is to help you gauge any job market changes regarding the skill in need and enable you to build an effective budget for the recruitment process.

Job Evaluation – This is where you compare the value of a job relative to other jobs within the organization, industry, and the job market. Job evaluation allows your organization to assess whether the employee is getting paid an amount proportionate to the required skills and qualifications. So, you need to first know the worth of the vacant position before rolling out an advertisement.

Once the recruitment plan is in place, sourcing for the right candidate becomes the next priority.

Talent Sourcing

Who do you want to recruit? Where can you get the best hands for the job? These are the essential questions you must answer during your recruitment process. Many applicants could seem like a good fit for the vacant position, but you need to find the right person. You are not hiring a crowd. You need an individual who fits perfectly for the vacant job, so talent sourcing is essential.

Talent sourcing involves identifying, researching, and networking with prospective candidates to discover the most suitable individual for the job out of all the other potential candidates. It is the process of selecting the most highly skilled applicant that fits your organization's value and culture.

You need to be selective and specific in talent sourcing. Otherwise, you might make the wrong judgment of the candidates. So, to avoid the mistakes, there are strategies you need for an effective talent sourcing process:

The Use of Job Boards

Many job seekers or people who intend to change jobs spend more time on job boards searching for a vacancy that fits their skills and experience. There are top job boards that are industry and skill-specific. You can target your prospective candidates through these means.

For instance, if your organization is within the health industry or the technology industry, you can selectively place a vacant position in that regard on the job board. When potential applicants search for jobs through these outlets, the applicants searching for these specific industries will find what they want through the job search engines.

The best job boards include Indeed, Google jobs, Monster, Craigslist, and so on. The <u>Indeed</u> job board is the most popular because it is a go-to that's free for many hiring managers searching for candidates.

The Social Media Tool (LinkedIn)

LinkedIn seems to be the most effective platform source for highly talented professionals among the many social media platforms. It is a networking platform that connects business owners with professionals who can do the job. Often, hiring managers look for the top candidates on LinkedIn since it permits them to see the prospective candidates' capabilities and interact with them in a more intimate yet professional way.

There are over 300 million users on LinkedIn, with a verified database for every LinkedIn profile. This makes it difficult for any individual to create a fake identity of his or her specific skills and job history. This is unlike other social media platforms like Facebook, Twitter, and Instagram, which are full of frauds. LinkedIn is the talent-sourcing platform for the future. As an HR manager, you will get the best from it.

Employee Referrals

Despite the vast age of a digitalized world, employee referrals still seem to be the most reliable and result-oriented way to source for pre-screen talents to fill a vacant job. Employees find it easy to recommend candidates within their network, especially when the hiring manager or the business owner rolls out compensation for the referral. So, if you need the best individual for the job, involve your employees in referral because this builds a higher level of trust and a higher percentage of job acceptance among applicants.

Recruitment Software

With the advent of technology, you can easily make data-driven decisions on job applications using recruitment software. This provides you with an easy route to the best candidate, based on programmed skills and vacant position requirements. Recruitment software automatically cuts out candidates whose résumés do not fit into the skillset or experience needed.

One advantage of the software is that it saves you time in the selection process and presents only qualified candidates. Most of this software does a background check, pre-assessment test, CV assessment, and recruitment analytics. The most common recruitment software used is the Applicant Tracking System (ATSs), Candidate Relationship Management (CRMs), and interviewing software like zoom.ai, sparks Hire, etc.

Horizontal and Vertical Promotion

Most of the time, the skills you need for a vacant position can be found in-house, but you may not know it. So, you must harness the potential of your employees by forming an internal promotion program. Help your employees attain higher job titles through horizontal promotion. At the same time, you can create more value for your company through training and knowledge expansion, also known as *horizontal promotion*. Promotion is not only a means to motivate your employees but also a talent sourcing strategy.

Internal Job Posting

Internally sourcing within your organization should also be one of your greatest strategies for talent sourcing. This is because you spend less on recruitment and onboarding when you allow interns or employees to fill vacant positions. Internal job posting builds trust between you and your employees, and it shows them you appreciate their career development.

An internal job advertisement isn't any different from what should be on the external job post, but you only limit the job post to your company's bulletin, newsletter, billboard, or intranet. This way, willing and qualified candidates can easily show their intention for the recruitment process.

Screening of Applicants

Now, the screening process is the next stage after talent sourcing. At this stage, you have a lot of candidates for the vacant job. Still, you need the most experienced and skilled applicant that fits your organization's structure and culture perfectly.

The screening process involves reviewing job applications to remove candidates less qualified for the job. This is where you examine and evaluate the applicant's skills and personality to affirm whether they are a good fit for the job.

You can also verify the candidate's referrals to determine if the candidate has a level of credibility and trust. Candidates might not have the work experience they claim to possess. Do a background check on the supposed employee to know if such a person has a haphazard employment history and any criminal record. The screening exercise might be time and energy-intensive, but it is worth it. You will have to check through a lot of cover letters and résumés to make your decision.

For companies using the application tracking system, this screening might have been done by the system. Still, you need to vet others further to find your ideal applicant.

There are five (5) things you must consider for an effective screening process. These are:

Relevant Experience

Applicants might have experience in several other jobs that are not relevant to your business. Many years of work experience do not equate to relevance to the position you are offering. So, you may have to choose between candidates working for many years versus someone employed fewer years – but with experience for the position you are offering.

Growth Factor

You must consider the growth potential of your applicants when screening. Certain jobs require years of relevant experience, but years of experience can also have limitations. For instance, how would you consider a candidate for a graduate trainee or junior position role that requires little or no work experience? Of course, the supposed candidate would be someone who would need to learn and grow on the job, so the age factor and career prospect will be better considerations than experience only.

Consider the Candidate's Availability

Everyone is busy. But we give priority to what is most important to us. Do any of the applicants keep switching their interview date during talent sourcing? Was the application late? Candidates like this might not eventually take the job. So, screen such people to avoid the problem of late resumption, especially when you need the right person to resume work immediately.

Pre-Screening Test

You must conduct a pre-screening test for the vacant position. The reason is that many applicants try to adjust their résumés to fit the vacant position, even though they do not have the requirement for the job. Conduct an aptitude test for the required skill. The test performance will show you whom to move further in the screening process.

Salary Requirement

You should not roll out a vacant position without a salary range. Your ideal candidate must be within your budget. Ask applicants their expected remuneration, as this is another way to screen the applicants.

These five considerations help you streamline your hiring process and choose who gets to sieve through the applications properly. The ultimate goal of every manager is to employ the best contender for his or her business. Sometimes, it can be difficult for an organization to attract the best candidates.

These factors can affect your organization in attracting the best candidates during the recruitment process:

The Structure of Your Organization Salary

Is your salary better than your competitors? Are there job benefits, bonuses, and incentive packages above the industry standard? The best candidates are naturally attracted to higher-paying organizations.

The Working Condition of Your Organization

Do you have proper facilities in your organization? Do you provide health care for your employees? Are your employees satisfied with their job? These are factors prospective candidates consider during the recruitment exercise. The best hand needs the best tools and a conducive work environment.

Business Reputation

An organization's reputation precedes itself. It either chases away prospective candidates or attracts the greatest. What is your organization known for? Do you care about your employees' personal and professional development? Is there job security in your organization? Your reputation matters when hunting the best candidates for a vacant position.

The screening stage is over when you have selected the candidate offered the job!

The Job Offer

In every recruitment process, the tedious stage is the screening of candidates. Once this stage is over, you are ready for the final stage. This is when the manager calls the selected candidate to be notified of the job offer. The notification is done via an offer letter to the selected employee.

An offer letter contains the following information: the start date, the conditions of employment, the work hours, and the compensation. Where the selected candidate declines, the whole recruitment process must start all over again!

Induction of the New Employee

As soon as your best candidate signs the employment contract and receives a welcome package, they are no longer a candidate and are now a new employee. During the induction phase, the manager introduces the employee to the existing staff. Induction does not automatically integrate the new employee into the culture of an organization. Onboarding is what the new employee needs.

Onboarding

Onboarding is the process of integrating new employees into the organization's work environment, culture, and practices.

How does onboarding differ from orientation?

Quite often, business owners find it difficult to differentiate between the process of onboarding a new employee and orientation. While the onboarding process requires employees to familiarize themselves with the company, orientation is the process where they learn about the company and their job duty.

Orientation is mostly about giving information about the job and the employee's role. This only happens in a day. An orientation process is a one-day event, unlike onboarding that takes weeks, a month, or sometimes the employee's first year on the job.

Purpose of Onboarding

- To make sure that the new employees feel accepted
- Makes a new employee feel at ease
- Creates a sense of belonging between the new entrant and old employees
- Helps new employees know what is expected of them
- Aids the new employee in understanding the organization, the culture, and the other staff
- Gives a new employee a platform to express his or her thoughts via feedback mechanisms

Certain components make an organization's onboarding program successful.

Welcoming the New Employee

Managers are usually busy, and they may consider it unnecessary to be around to welcome their new employees. You need to make it a habit to be there to welcome and introduce the new employee to the rest of the staff.

You can also give the new employee access to the organization's employee page on the website. This will help them acclimatize with the organization's culture.

Organization Introduction

The introduction can be in a video or an oral presentation. It provides an outline of the organization's objective, mission, and vision to the new employee. It could also be an opportunity to reiterate the function of the new employee as it relates to the goals of the organization.

Policies and Procedures

Your organization can accomplish this through employees' orientation or by providing an organization handbook to the new employee.

Cultural Integration

Cultural integration helps the new employee seamlessly integrate into the organization's culture. For instance, you are to make sure that they know the structure of the office, such as where the bathroom, water cooler, coffee machine, and supply room are.

Mentorship

The need for proper mentorship is crucial to help new employees master their roles promptly. The HR manager should assign mentors to help them understand the nature of the job and the organization's workplace culture.

Onboarding Tips

- Make sure that the rest of the office knows that a new employee will be joining them.
- Have a swag bag prepared to welcome your new employee. The swag bag could contain organization logo t-shirts, candy, a bottle of water, a small gift card, etc.
- Order lunch in for the whole staff on the new employee's first day at work. This will help them, and the current employees become better acquainted.
- Give the new employee small tasks to do in the first few days of work.

Applicants Tracking System (ATS) Integration Tools

These integrations will allow you to facilitate many of the managerial aspects of the onboarding process. It will free up your time to focus on the larger task at hand.

Checkr: It is used to check the background of your candidates during screening.

DocuSign: It's used to create, send, and receive letters and job contracts with signatures electronically.

Blackbirding: It is used to welcome new employees. You can welcome your new employees with a video, office map, and any other content, using this tool.

21st Century Recruitment Tips

Use Google Ad Words

The Google Ad word is used to place text-based ads on job boards. This will enable you to place ads for keywords that your prospective candidates might be searching for. You can direct them back to the job posting on your site.

Profile Your Company's Best

Profile your best employees and aim for similar candidates. You can use their virtues as a guide for assessing other candidates.

Target niche-based job boards like the BigShoes network. This is a marketing website, unlike the general job boards like Indeed, Monster, CareerBuilder, etc.

Display what makes your work culture great.

For instance, this can be your working hours, unique benefits, and staff relationship.

Create a mentoring program.

Since the older employees have a wealth of experience, they can transfer their knowledge to the newer employees.

Create a Database

Make your recruitment process data-driven. For instance, identify through which channel your candidates come in and through which channel you get the most successful employees.

Use Virtual Reality

Organizations are using a virtual reality experience in recruitment techniques. Your organization can use this to show candidates they are in an exciting and innovative workplace. It gives your candidates a realistic view of the office and of the organization's culture.

Chapter 5: Performance Management Strategies

The overall desire of every organization is to win in the marketplace. But you cannot succeed in the market unless you first win in your workplace. How can your organization do that? It is simple and easy. You need to align your employees' roles with the organization's goal. To do that, you need to evaluate and gauge the performance of your employees periodically.

Every organization must learn how to evaluate and assess their employees' performance to stay ahead of competitors. This performance assessment should be based on roles that clearly relate to the organization's goal. This is a shift from the traditional yearly assessment. This concept is called *performance management.*

What is Performance Management?

Performance management aims to optimize employee performance by offering a frequent reward system for employees to increase their efficiency and that of the organization. It harmonizes their role in an organization in the same direction of the organization's purpose and objectives. Briefly, it is a summation of individual performances as they align to accomplish the big picture of the organization's goal. Let's look at the big picture.

Performance management means you support the constant development of your employees so they meet the company's goals by remaining consistent in their tasks. The strategies and useful techniques that the **HR** manager employs include onboarding, training, and developing employees, then checking out feedback from the employee.

Lately, business owners and **HR** managers have realized that yearly employee appraisal does not work. It had become an old strategy to motivate people to work. Appraisal no longer motivates employees to carry out their tasks because it takes too long for it to reward the worker's effort.

You cannot determine an employee's performance just through simple appraisal. Effective performance management strategies become necessary to analyze a workers' performance.

Why is Performance Management Important?

All organization needs to know their workers intimately. You need to check out what your employees do, why they do it, and how they do it. A business owner cannot understand all that it takes to run the business without having a system in place. This system will review the employee's weaknesses and strengths, document any feedback given, and reward a positive attitude on the job.

A good organization rewards the excellent performance of employees. They have a reward system for employees who carry out their duties and help the company reach its goals.

Importance of Performance Management

Human resources is an important part of every organization. They are responsible for what works within the company, so you must know how to manage this effectively. Businesses find it hard to manage this because they struggle with knowing how to achieve the following:

- How to keep employees engaged
- How to retain talents
- How to groom leaders from within the organization
- How to align organizational goals with employee's goals
- How to reward good performance and identify poor performance
- How to manage feedback
- How to ease the danger of discrimination and favoritism

Now, let's look at the ten benefits that performance management can give to your organization:

Setting Goals Becomes Easier

Performance management helps to align the company's goals with the employees ' goals. Often, a yearlong appraisal plan fails because it does not allow employees to work in real-time. But when you schedule a rewarding process for periodic goals, employees perform well since they see job success as a part of their plans.

Measuring Employee's Performance Becomes Easier

Performance management is a strategy to track progress on goals. It allows you to easily monitor the pace of tasks using metrics and analytics.

Training Employees Becomes Easier

When your organization creates a system for measuring employees' performance, it becomes easier to know exactly which area they need improvement and training.

It Becomes Easier for an Organization to Stay Relevant

Employees enjoy receiving reviews and feedback on their tasks in real-time. This facilitates them to make adjustments where necessary while they keep up with market changes. The organization stays relevant if they can navigate through the business market.

It Boosts Organization Reputation

Employees trust your organizations more when you reward them for their performance. They will begin to see the organization as an entity that cares and recognizes their effort.

It Increases Organization Output

Constantly engaging employees through frequent review of performance and feedback increases your organization's output. According to research by Gallup, organizations that involve their employees in performance-related business outcomes experience a 240% boost compared to those who do not.

It Becomes Easier for the Organization to Groom Leaders

Performance management helps you identify potential leadership traits in your employees through training and career development. Employees that are trained become an asset to your organization. Employees stay when they receive professional development and/or a reward for their performance.

It Increases Employee's Engagement

Frequent feedback and mentoring keep employees focused on their work. According to Forbes, companies that set performance goals quarterly generate 31% greater returns from their performance process.

It Boosts Talent Retention

Employees who enjoy both personal and professional development from your organization will want to stay with the organization.

It Identifies and Solves Problems Quickly

Frequent review of employee's performance supports quick identification of problems and fast intervention.

These and many more are the benefits, but the strategy you employ for successful performance management becomes our next consideration.

Strategies in Performance Management

Below are seven strategies for effective performance management:

- Goal Setting
- Pre-emptive management
- Review and Feedback
- Assessment
- Grading Scale
- Training
- Reward and Compensation

Goal Setting

Employee's performances are measured using the organization's goals as a benchmark. An organization without a clear goal is as bad as an organization without a goal. As a manager or a business owner, you must set goals for your employees. Goals are like a road map for the employees to follow to accomplish their tasks and for the organization to fulfill its purpose.

The goal of your organization has to be clear, concise, and attainable. It should not be ambiguous, and employees should be able to interpret it effortlessly. Once the employee buys into the organization's goal, it will be easier for them to interpret the goal in relation to their tasks and role.

The collective roles of the employees in an organization are channeled towards the common goal of the organization. This drives the organization towards winning in the marketplace.

Pre-Emptive Management

The idea behind pre-emptive management is all about communicating your goals and expectations to your employees. It also encompasses how your employees can meet these goals and expectations. You are to set aside regular meetings with them to see how they are working on their goals.

Review and Feedback

There is a need to check an employee's performance once an organization makes its plan and sets its goal. The essence of the review is to see how your employees are performing. You want to make sure that they are doing what is expected of them.

Explain to them the importance of reviews. When a review is interactive, your employees will not just see it as another stressful task they have to endure. Once they see the review as an avenue for them to discuss their perspective, they will embrace it.

Reviews should be done, remembering that you want to make sure your employees have not lost focus on the goals set before them.

Besides, the review process makes it possible to keep track of your organization's goals and reward an employee's performance. As an HR manager, make sure that you get timely and frequent feedback from employees. You can use performance software, Google forums, or Survey Monkey to collect feedback after each review meeting.

Assessment

The organization's assessment of the employees is to see how well they are performing and where they will likely need improvement. Assessment assists you in making sure that you do not have a square peg in a round hole. While assessing them, avoid the temptation of blaming them for not performing to your expectations. This only breaks their spirit and lowers their morale.

The reason for the assessment is not to make your employees feel bad and incompetent. Always make it an avenue for them to improve on any incompetency. You need to focus more on the positive measures they need to take to improve themselves.

Grading Scale

The grading scale helps to grade employees' performance. A grading scale is just a scale used to define performance level – however you see fit. For instance, let us say the numbering on the grading scale is from one to three.

The number one could indicate that the employee does not perform very well. (Employee needs skill training).

The number two could suggest that the employee performs averagely. (Employee needs to improve).

The number three could mean that the employee performs to expectation.

It becomes easier to identify where your employees stand with this grading system. You know who to go for more training, and the ones to be rewarded.

Training

The essence of training is to make sure that the employees have the right skills for their role in the organization. You can also optimize an employee's performance through additional skills training. Training offers development opportunities for your employees.

You can train your entire staff in human relations, mentorship, marketing, use of sophisticated machines, leadership, etc. But the training will depend on the employees' roles and will also depend on how the roles collectively positively affect the organization's goal. The training can be in in-house training, online resources, or professional training.

The end result of training your employees are numerous. Because you are boosting their morale and your organization's reputation, it is a win-win situation.

Rewards and Compensation

It is a natural occurrence to link reward and compensation to good performance. Implementing rewards and incentives is a way to show employees you see their efforts and that you are pleased with their performance.

Incentivizing performance keeps employees motivated, and they are made aware that you want them to keep up their good performance. There are several ways to reward performance and maintain motivation. These include:

- Salary increases
- Bonus
- Shares in the organization
- A seat on the organization's board
- Extra holidays
- Promotion
- Recognition

The strategies stated above are to make sure that your organization performs optimally. Performance management should lead to organizational success and employees' growth.

Real-World Business Examples of Performance Management

Performance management is not just a "theory thing." It has a solid application in real-time business. Several corporations built their organization as a result of effective strategies. Below are a few of these companies for your consideration:

Google

Google is the foremost company in the tech industry. It builds its performance strategy on data analysis and training. Google is very keen on training their managers to allow them to lead the future of the tech industry.

Facebook

This is another huge company within the tech industry. Facebook emphasizes peer-to-peer feedback as one of their performance strategies. Periodically, they send out a survey to their users to help analyze their employees' performances. Through this, the company understands what is working and what is not. One major aspect of Facebook's performance strategy is the generation of real-time feedback from their customers.

Adobe

Adobe managers had to switch from the traditional yearly appraisal to real-time check-ins on their employees. This company's management realized that employees felt discouraged even after managers had spent over 80,000 hours a year on performance reviews. This affected the company's turnover rate before the company changed to a frequent check-in program.

Performance Management Best Practices in HRM

I. What do you want to accomplish with your performance management program?

- Is it to reward or to recognize employees?
- Is it to guarantee that your organization's goals are met?
- Is it to identify and solve problems?

II. Once you understand what your performance management program sets out to accomplish, then you need to define your employees' roles. This will help them know exactly what they are expected to do.

III. The review becomes important once the employees' role has been aligned with the organization's goal. By using metrics and analytics, you can track how goals are progressing.

IV. Creating guidelines for your employees' roles helps them do a better job.

V. Rewarding employees keeps them motivated to do more. Recognize and compensate your employees for their performance.

VI. Training the trainer programs should be embraced by an organization. This will make certain that the managers are professionally trained in managerial skills.

Performance Management Tools

There are several digital tools essential to check an employee's performance. Some of these include:

- Applicant Tracking System - It is utilized to improve the recruitment process.
- Goal alignment software - It is needed to manage projects, meetings, and tasks.

- HR Competencies - It articulates and identifies excellence in the organization.

- Role Management - It is used to give the employee role its own goals.

- Goal tracking Software - It is adopted to define and outline goals.

- Virtual Team Building- It supports teammates bonding together from remote places.

- Artificial Intelligence - It utilizes A.I., like chatbots, to evaluate employees' performance.

Chapter 6: Payroll, Compensation, and Benefits

In the early 1920s, researchers and business owners came to the foreknowledge of Human Resources Management. The human resource department's function mainly concentrated on transactional work, such as payroll and benefits administration.

What is Payroll?

Payroll is a listed document that contains the record of a company's employees and staff, which is used to process each employee's paycheck. This payment might fall on the same day or different days for the employees, either as wages or salaries.

With the advancement of technology, software called Payroll Management System (PMS) was created to ease the job of every HR manager in dispensing payment of all employees in any organization. The PMS allows for the management of both permanent and contract employees' payrolls in the payroll cycle.

Payroll Cycle

A payroll cycle is the length of time that circulates between payrolls. This task starts with a particular step and ends with another, continuously repeating, and therefore managing the employee workforce's pay effectively.

Discharging of employees (firing) is an activity performed sometimes; It is not a repeated cycle (like every other activity mentioned in the previous paragraph.)

In payrolls, deductions in salaries and wages occur for different reasons:

- Health Insurance
- State income taxes
- Social security taxes
- Federal income taxes
- Charitable contributions
- Local tax withholdings, etc.

Below is the relevance of the payroll cycle to your organization:

- Payroll information can prepare the budget for the company's expenditure.
- It helps in the accuracy and effectiveness of financial reporting.
- It is essential for legal compliance, e.g., tax and labor laws.

Human Resource Management and Payroll Activities

The HR manager oversees the major payroll activities of the business. Here, there are a few correlations between the HR manager and payroll activities in the company.

- The HR manager produces up-to-date Master Data of the employees and their payments.
- They are in charge of termination and changes in pay rates that reflect on the payroll.
- Employee's information on time and attendance varies in the way they receive their paychecks. Therefore, the HR manager confirms each employee's entry and exit to coordinate the correct payment.
- They are in charge of preparing payroll.
- They distribute the payroll through different channels and payment portals to every employee.
- They coordinate distributing taxes and miscellaneous deductions.

Interestingly, there are many threats to payroll. If not adequately checked, these are a financial risk liability to the business accounts and data. It includes inaccurate or invalid master data, unauthorized access, fraud in disbursement, inaccurate recording, violation of employment laws, etc.

Many companies outsource the payroll functions to organizations or companies that deal with Payroll duties on a significant scale to avoid unnecessary imbalance, stress, and workload. Some of these outsourcing options are Payroll Service Bureau and Professional Employer Organizations.

Pros and Cons of Outsourcing Payroll Services

Hiring the service of a professional payroll through outsourcing has two sides to it. So, it depends on what you prefer for your business. Most business owners hire a professional payroll service to save the organization the rigor of collecting data for payments. They do this so the organization can focus on what is most important and grow internally.

A professional payroll also simplifies the company's accounting procedures so it does not negate the legal and tax filing required. A disadvantage of outsourcing the payroll service is that the consequence of errors does fall on the HR manager in charge. Your employee will fault you for any mistake and not the professional you hire to work on the payroll. Also, if this error affects the tax, the company might have to pay for this mistake. So, you must choose wisely how to outsource your payroll services.

Compensation

Compensation is considered the primary pillar of why a person (an employee) works for a firm. It is one of the vital parts of Human Resources Management, helps encourage employees, and improves organizational effectiveness.

Compensation can be defined as the approach a business owner adopts by giving monetary value or non-monetary value to their employees. This is done as a sign of appreciation to employees for their hard work.

According to Keith Davis, compensation is what employees receive in exchange for their contribution to the organization. It includes payments like sales commission, bonuses, profit sharing, overtime pay, recognition rewards, etc. It could also include non-monetary perks like a company-paid car, company-paid housing, stock opportunities, and the like.

In building a successful business, there has to be the stability of loyal employees, and in doing so, employers devise a means of attracting, motivating, and retaining employees. This comprises key components that can help complete the employers' strategy. They are:

• Base pay: It involves wages and salaries received by employees. It is the result of every given service of an employee to the organization.

- Commissions: Any financial incentive payment or reward attained or received by an employee for carrying out duties efficiently and effectively.

- Overtime pay: This is usually given to the employees who have worked more hours than initially scheduled and can include additional functions and duties different from what has been earlier agreed upon.

- Bonuses and Profit sharing: These are added values to an employee based on the company's profit or organization. These mostly happen on a special occasion and after a profitable year within the company.

- Allowances: This is not considered in an employee's base pay. They are given to employees to cover added expenses they would not normally incur during their assigned workday. This additional payment will allow them something to hold them for a while until they get their fixed pay.

- Recognition rewards: These kinds of compensation are often given and credited to an employee on merit. They are mostly given to show appreciation for their daily dedication and sincerity to work.

There are two core elements that compensation encompasses, and they are:

- Fixed pay- It is a base pay that is constant and doesn't vary.

- Variable pay- This pay changes based on the performance, efforts, and results of an employee to the organization.

Business owners do not just give rewards to employees without plans to counter-balance it. This plan would help you provide total rewards to employees and still make your profit in business. It is another function and duty of the Human Resources Management department to make compensation plans.

There are various ways or theories you, as an HR manager, can use to develop a compensation plan. Three elements make up building a basic model plan. These three elements are internal alignment, external competitiveness, and compensation management. Each element embodies steps that can help in proper planning.

Internal Alignment

Internal alignment covers job analysis, job evaluation, pay policy, and identification of the organization's different employees. This concerns the organization's internal dealings, like their detailed structure, functions, purposes, etc. It helps in distinguishing between employees, their different duties, and their pay. Consequently, each employee's pay varies according to his or her different functions and duties.

For example, every company or organization's different department carries out different duties, and yet, they are all putting forth an effort to make the company grow. Those in the Human Resources Management department's functions are dissimilar from those in the Accounting department, which means their pay and bonuses are also different.

There are seven steps, and they are categorized differently under the following elements.

1. Job Analysis: It covers job descriptions and a job's documentation. The analysis of each job in an organization identifies the similarities and differences in work. It sheds light on what an employee's job duties are all about and provides the employee a clear idea of what is paid for.

2. Job Evaluation: It is a methodical way to decide the value and worth of a job in relation to jobs in other companies. In the job evaluation, there should be a degree of analysis to produce a detailed and concise understanding of the job.

Certain processes should be adhered to to generate a quality job evaluation.

- The job in question must have gained acceptance. Meaning, the top management of an organization must explain the aims and uses of the program or job to the managers while emphasizing the benefits.

- There should be a committee created solely to evaluate the key jobs of the organization. This committee should include HR experts and experienced employees in the company.

- There should be research to find the key job to evaluate in a company. Every job need not be assessed since it could be too tasking and cumbersome.

- There should be analysis and preparation of the job description.

- There should also be a selection made for evaluation methods, which adheres to the company's culture and policies.

3. Pay Policy: This is a deliberate and concise decision of a company that determines if they want to lead, meet, or lag the market in compensation. To lead the market is for you to make your pay rates higher than the market price or place. To meet is to make sure their rates are comparable to the relative marketplace. To lag is when the rates are below the relative marketplace.

External Competitiveness

External competitiveness is more or less a wage competition between an organization and its competitors and rivals. Here, research is done to discover the compensation being offered by your competitors. This is solely to make a pay comparison to know how to pay your employee.

This method puts the HR manager in the middle of this competition where they recruit the best employees, train, and retain them. It becomes a bid of "who pays more gets the best." You can do this in two ways:

• Market Analysis: This is also called market pricing, and it can be accomplished in three steps. These steps include selecting data, using the age data, and using the weight data.

• Base Pay Structure: It is the initial and actual salary paid to an employee without benefits, bonuses, and raises. It is the value they receive in exchange for their services. The organization looks into rival companies to work their way around their base pay structure, in order not to lag behind in the marketplace.

Compensation Management

It is the general overview of managing a company's compensation structure based on its policies and procedures. It can also be called wage and salary administration. There is an implementation of variable pay, which is concerned with designing and implementing total compensation packages. There is also a pact that enforces and confirms that employees understand their compensations according to the way it varies.

Compensation management has its own aim and objectives for the company. Below are a few:

1. Acquiring qualified personnel

2. Retaining of company's employees

3. Checks and balances on cost and the company's budget

4. Facilitate understanding of employees and employers

5. Rewarding of desired and appropriate behavior of employees

6. To make sure the company and organization comply with legal regulations

Also, you can do this in two ways:

• Pay for Performance: Payment for employees' performance in their various duties and functions should be made without delay.

• Communicate the Plan: This is the last step in compensation planning. The compensation plans need to be communicated to employees. Business owners must also make sure that they understand their plan and have a clear line of sight between organization mission, culture, and compensation.

Employee Benefits

Employee benefits are the additional bonuses and compensation, aside from hourly wages and salaries, which an employee receives from the management of his or her organization. The list of employee benefits includes:

- Health Insurance
- Life Insurance
- Dental Insurance
- Paid time off- sick days and vacation days
- Retirement benefits
- Childcare benefits
- Tuition reimbursements
- Bonuses or incentives
- Gym and Club Memberships
- Healthcare spending
- Social security
- Disability insurance and many more

Employee benefits go a long way in building a company because they feel like the company supports them. An employee benefit helps in attracting and retaining talents. It shows that the organization cares for its staff's wellbeing, and the benefits give an organization an edge over its competitors. Also, it causes an increase in focus, dedication, productivity, and loyalty of the employee to the company.

Difference Between Payroll and Compensation

Payroll and compensation (benefits) may bear similarities in the sense they both serve as a payment (monetary and non-monetary value) given for the dedicated service of an employee to the company or organization. But this does not mean they are the same. Employers and employees should know there is a clear difference between the two. An employee could be paid both compensations and benefits, but not without the back up of a payroll.

As earlier stated, the primary function of payroll is the distribution of paychecks to employees at their different pay times. Then, payrolls can also be called the accounting of wages, salaries, and other payouts within company budgets and finances.

Payroll involves the payment of basic pay, but compensation goes broader than that since it generally refers to all kinds of pay that goes to an organization's employee. Compensation covers the payment of total rewards, bonuses, recognition rewards, etc.

Payroll is the process that includes the preparation of valid payroll worksheets and checks. It contains the total pay for each employee of various functions, and it deducts essential income taxes and deductions for other sole purposes. Compensation is the end result of whatever has been deducted and subtracted.

In each payroll, employees get a payroll statement covering every detail of the pay, be it daily wages, weekly wages, or salaries. Compensation statements come occasionally, and when given, it will provide every record of the pay, benefits, and rewards given earlier to an employee. It can be bi-monthly or annually, all based on the structure and system of the organization.

Chapter 7: Maintaining Positive Employee Relations (ER)

Businesses thrive on the interaction between business owners and their employees. Your manner of communication with your employee as a business owner or HR manager has a significant effect on your business and the workplace culture. So, maintaining positive employee relations (ER) effectively boosts your workers' enthusiasm to work, which minimizes conflict among coworkers and increases business productivity.

What are Employee Relations?

Employee Relations (ER) is defined as the positive relationship between an employer or HR manager and their employees.

ER focuses on how to manage the employer-employee relationship to garner employees' best performance on their job. This helps boost their morale to work, and in turn, increases the company's productivity. So, the growth of an organization depends on how HR managers or business owners treat their employees as paid workers and as stakeholders in the company.

In times past, businesses settled disputes at the industrial courts. This traditional means of resolving problems created more problems within the organizations because most companies found relief from the trade union, labor union, and government agencies against employees. That weakened the relationship between business owners and employees. Measures were taken to bridge the gap between these two parties. So, ER was introduced into the Human Resource Management department of every organization.

The ER is primarily to prevent and settle disputes among workers and between the management and employees. There are various reasons for conflicts in any organization. For example, salary delay, undue termination of appointment, breach of contracts, unreasonable working hours, favoritism, and so on, are a few of the causes of dispute in the workplace.

Employee Relations management comes as a solution to eradicate or minimize the phenomenon of industrial disputes in the workplace. Business owners and managers now understand that the growth of their company depends heavily on the company's workforce.

Subsequently, ER ensures that the company's policies are fair to its employees and not just in favor of the management alone. If your employees are happy with their job, they will gladly participate and increase productivity. The concept of ER is to enact policies that encourage workers' passion for their job. These policies range from health and safety to insurance programs that benefit your company.

Treat your workers as kings, and they will, in turn, make your customers feel like kings. Treat them with dignity and value, and they will respond likewise to your customers. Your employee reflects your company's image, either positively or negatively. They respond to others as you treat them. If you do not value them, they will never place a premium on your customer or clients. So, maintaining a good work-friendly relationship with your employee is key to your company's sales and growth.

Realize that alone, you cannot do much in your company. But together, you can achieve more. Your company will function at its peak when more hands contribute effectively to the smooth function of the business. But how would you involve more people to enhance productivity if you do not have a strong ER as a manager?

How to Build Strong Employee Relationships

Top CEOs of multinational companies have learned the powerful effect of ER on their organization. This is why Tim Cook of Apple Inc. creates time to engage employees in discussions by eating lunch with them. Jean-Paul Agon of L'Oréal Group eats with employees in the cafeteria or break room. Also, co-founder and CEO of Fullcontact Inc, Bart Lorang, offers an annual all paid vacation of $7,500 to their employees to use as they like.

One common thing among these employers is that they relate with their employees on a personal level. Attitudes like these enhance a positive employee relationship. Below are the major considerations for building strong employee relations:

- **Create a Positive Workplace Condition for Your Employees**

Are your employees happy with the condition of their workplace? Do your employees love their job? Are they able to balance their work and life? How flexible are their work schedules?

Only 42% of the US employees are eager to work every day, compared to 84% of the best 100 companies to work within America. This report is according to a 2019 Fortune Top 100 report.

Flexible work hours and work environment are essential to building a strong ER in your organization. Just as the words of Judy Village, the president of the Association of Canadian Ergonomists, explained that a positive workplace condition is not about the physical environment. It is also the office culture that fits the employees' cognitive and psychological needs.

Your company's work culture should not be toxic to your employee. Create a healthy relationship where they can easily express their feelings without fear or prejudice. Be a leader, not someone to fear. By showing compassion and empathy to your employees anytime they need help, this will make them trust you more and they will become more committed to the job.

- **Provide Job Benefits and Rewards**

Besides the salary, what other benefits do your employees enjoy? Is there any plan for their health? Do you have programs that encourage hard work and dedication? What about expenses for your employees' vacation plans? These benefits are significant ways to show your appreciation to them for their contribution to your company. Benefits and rewards for employees show that you value them and recognize their contribution.

Most companies now adopt policies that allow their employees to work from the comfort of their homes, especially given the recent pandemic situation. You can do this too. But remember that the aim is to foster a strong and healthy employee-employer relationship.

- **Create Goals with Your Employees**

It is not unusual for the HR manager to draft out plans and objectives on their own and then delegate duties according to these plans. This is not actually the wrong thing to do. But a business that desires more growth must seek more employee involvement. Sometimes, you do not have to create goals single-handedly. You can involve them as well since the goals are about what each employee will be doing for the week or month. So, plan with them not for them.

Often, employees have ideas that will work better than what you might have implemented while goal setting yourself. You must always make sure that the goals you create with your employees align with the company's values and objectives to avoid conflicting goals.

- **Career Development**

Employees feel happier when they have a goal to pursue, especially if it is one that helps further their career. Always find ways to help them grow in their jobs. This could be a mentorship program and leadership training. You could also organize cross-sectional training that will allow them to learn skills from other departments, which will help them in multiple roles.

- **Communication**

Communication is one way an organization can function well. You give employees tasks, and they report back to you. Coworkers work together through communication, and this further enhances excellent workplace relations. But business owners have realized there is a need for non-work communication to improve employee relations.

Sometimes, you need to talk with your employees about personal issues. Ask about their goals and play fun games together. This method of informal communication brings unity to the organization and, consequently, teamwork. Encourage your employees to share their personal lives, beliefs, and values with one another. Be open with them so they can confide in you, even with personal matters, about their lives.

The Power of Positive Employee Relations

HR managers and business owners should now realize that improving positive ER in the workplace does a great deal to the organization. Gone are the days where employees just go to work just for the paycheck. These days, workers seek cognitive, social, and psychological satisfaction. Since the workplace is where they spend most of their time, employees feel fulfilled when they find what they seek there. This satisfaction can be possible only when you encourage positive relationships.

A review by Harvard Business School revealed that about 60% of employees said a positive relationship with their employer significantly affected their level of productivity. 44% reported that a positive relationship boosted overall performance on their job.

This is to say that positive employee relationships affect not only the employee but also the business as a whole. Here are the advantages of positive employee relations in the workplace:

- **Increase Presence at Work**

In a situation where your employees love and enjoy their work, coming to work becomes something they look forward to every day. Ideally, coming in late to work or absenteeism will no longer be an issue for discussion. Of course, regular work attendance boosts your organization's productivity because when all hands are on deck, everyone works towards the same goal more efficiently.

- **Change of Attitude to Work**

Employees' satisfaction with their job creates a positive outlook at work. They will love new challenges and will likely go above and beyond to achieve any workplace task. A positive ER creates that outlook among employees.

- **Skill Retention**

Skill retention has become a significant concern for business owners due to the hiring process's cost. So, having a new employee quit shortly after being hired becomes a serious problem for the company. But then, why would an employee quit if he or she finds satisfaction with the job?

According to a report by Strategic Human Resources, it was reported that employees find satisfaction in their job because of the positive relationship with their immediate supervisor or senior managers.

- **Improve Employee Motivation**

Everybody wants to be treated well and appreciated for his or her efforts. Employees are more motivated to do more when you, as their manager or business owner, appreciate their efforts, no matter how little they might be. Simple words like "thank you" can sometimes be enough to motivate your employees to do more!

- **The Workplace Becomes a Home**

Employee relations bring understanding and harmony to the workplace. Your organization becomes a work family, where employees see themselves as one big family.

- **It Boosts the Organization's Reputation**

If you want positive feedback about your brand, then you can show it by the way you treat your employees. Organizations with positive employee relations do enjoy a boost in their reputations. Good work benefits, health care insurance, rewards, and recognition culture are ways you can boost your organization's reputation.

- **Improves Efficiency**

Employee relations improve efficiency through employee skills training and in-house courses. You improve the employee's efficiency through the ways you train them on the job.

Now that you know the powerful benefits of positive ER, how do you, as a business owner or a manager, plan to achieve this? The ER power is not a one-time feat; it takes multiple processes.

What are Employee Relations Processes?

Employee relation processes are methods or approaches that HR managers adopt to handle issues regarding employees in the workplace. The process, which used to be industrial relations, is an approach used to settle disputes between management and employees. There are different approaches to employee relations processes. You can choose any approach of your choice depending on the uniqueness of your business or organization.

- Adversaries Approach: This is an approach where the management makes the decisions for employees to comply with. Employees have no say in the company. The only way they could exercise their power is to oblige the company's decision.

- Traditional Approach: In this approach, the management of an organization only relates to an elected representative of the employees, not the general workforce.

- Partnership Approach: By this approach, the organization involves employees in decision making, especially in creating policies. But the sole right to manage these policies resides with the management alone.

- Power Sharing: This is an approach whereby both management and the employees are involved in making decisions that concern the daily running of the business.

Now, to appreciate the employee relation processes, we will look into the employee relations' policies and employee relations' strategies.

Employee Relations Policies

Employee relations' policies convey the relationships between business managers or owners, employees, and preferred trade unions and how to handle such relationships.

These policies express what an organization needs to do to guide its present and future decisions. It also expresses what course of action to change in the way an organization manages its employee relations and its relationship with the supposed union.

Every organization has its own employee relations policies that express how it deals with issues about its employees and the unions. This involves:

- **Union Recognition**

You can choose whether to recognize unions when it comes to conditions for employment in your company. But if you choose to recognize a union to bargain as the trade union, then they must represent your employees for collective bargaining.

There are two kinds of recognition. It could be full recognition, whereby the union has a representation and negotiation right. Or, it could be partial recognition, whereby the union only represents the employee. In partial recognition, the union discusses nothing that concerns employment.

- **Collective Bargaining**

Collective bargaining involves two parties. These are the business owner and the unions. The two parties come together to reach an agreement regarding conditions for employment and how to resolve disputes, grievances, and disciplinary issues. The agreement is done in two ways - the Substantive agreement and the Procedural agreement. Substantive agreements are not legally binding to you as the business owner, and include agreements such as pay and work hours, holidays, allowances, overtime regulations, and work flexibility.

As the name implies, procedural agreements are procedures that organizations need to follow in collective bargaining and in resolving industrial disputes.

- **Participation and Involvement**

It explains to what length a company is prepared to involve its employees in decision-making, especially matters that concern them. This way, employees can share their ideas and their opinions about their work.

- **Partnership Agreement**

It explains to what length an organization thinks it can partner with its employees.

Employee Relations Best Practices

These best practices are human management strategies you can adopt to manage relationships with your employees effectively. If you endeavor to put them into practice, it will create a comparative advantage for you over your competitors. Below are the employee relations' best practices you need.

- **Communication**

The key to a lasting and enjoyable relationship is honest communication. The same applies to the employer-employee relationships. Whatever you need to communicate with your employees, either the organization's vision, goals, or tasks, make sure it is clear, concise, and understandable.

Attempt to build a friendly but professional relationship with your employees. Make them feel at ease and unafraid to ask you questions.

- **Make the Organization's Vision Memorable**

Every employee in your organization should know the company's values and what it stands for. Let your employees know their duty towards making the company goal a reality. Show them both in words and action what the company vision is and encourage them to buy into the vision.

The simplest way to imprint the company's vision into your employees' hearts is to make it a commonplace phenomenon in the office. You can imprint it on office stationery, office coffee mugs, cards, glass, etc. Make sure that the vision is visible everywhere in the office. Thus, wherever the employees look, they will see the vision boldly written there.

- **Trust Your Employees Ability to Perform**

Once you have communicated the organization's vision clearly to your employees and believe they can relate it to their roles within the organization, the next thing to do is simply watch them from afar.

You need to trust your employee to do the work by giving them the autonomy of the work. Do not micromanage them because they will find it annoying, and it will make them feel as though you do not trust them.

- **Appreciation and Recognition**

Nobody wants to remain where he or she is not valued. You need to show your employees you care for them and value their contribution to your business's progress. This attitude builds strong employee relations. Appreciation can come in various forms. It could be a note of thanks, a promotion at work, gifts, thank-you card, email, etc. Your appreciation encourages them to do more.

- **Make the Employees Part of the Decision Making**

Ask for your employees' suggestions and ideas. Let them know that they have a say in the organization too. They should see themselves as stakeholders in your company. Listen to them and act on their words, as long as it correlates with the company's goals.

- **Make Corporate Social Responsibility (CSR) Relevant**

How are your organization's policies and procedures? Are they employee-friendly? Make sure your organization involves its host community in its policies and procedures. This will help to dissuade community disputes, especially if your organization is into production.

Create policies and procedures that take care of the community's needs local to your business. Small or medium companies must contribute to developing the location where their business is situated. Set aside a Corporate Social Responsibility (CSR) department in your organization. Also, make sure that your organization's policies and procedures take care of your employees' welfare.

- **Have Competitive Wages and Salaries Structures**

High-paying organizations tend to have a higher employee retention rate compared to low-paying ones. But organizations that pay well have a higher percentage of talented professionals working with them. Make sure your organization pays more than your competitors pay. That way, you will have a comparative advantage of the best skills and most talented people working with you.

- **Encourage In-House Skills Development**

Skills and character development programs in an organization will discourage employees from seeking assistance from unions and government agencies. Your company should organize skills and training programs for its employees. Training improves the performance of employees at work.

- **Implement the Use of Software**

Using software removes undue stress and redundant tasks from the workplace. There is software that your organization can use that makes work easier for the employees and removes repetitive tasks. Some of these are project management software, messaging software, and recruitment software, which makes office work seamless and hassle-free.

Your ER is a huge aspect of your company that determines how far it will go. Your business's future, which is likely of great concern to you, hinges on developing a positive ER with your employees, so it's wise to invest your time and effort into it.

Chapter 8: Legal Considerations

There is a propensity or likelihood of a conflict of interest or a dispute in every human relationship. Although this will not annul the purpose of the relationship, it shows differences in perspective and perception. To minimize the tendency of conflict in the workplace, the HR managers or business owner needs to understand the legal bindings of work in the organization. The legal aspect of your business regulates any form of excesses or inadequacies among employees.

But you must not leave the legal aspect to the company's attorney alone. As an HR manager, you have a role to play. You need to consider legal issues in making policies that affect the business and your employees. Understanding employer-employee relationships will guide you in creating policies that will prevent lawsuits and other legal actions against this workplace relationship.

Aside from your roles in recruitment, onboarding, and payroll, you also need to understand the relevant business laws. These laws guide workers in the workplace if a conflict occurs, occupational hazards, and other environmental factors that affect the organization.

Here are the legal issues you need to consider as an HR manager or business owner with employee relations and workplace policies.

Discrimination Charges

An employee might be denied a job, a course, or skill training for reasons that are not relevant in the workplace. Although the employee might not be eligible for such, finding unnecessary reasons to deny them is discrimination and a legal issue in the workplace. These discrimination charges can take these forms:

- Gender discrimination
- Racial discrimination
- Sexual discrimination
- Religion discrimination
- Marital discrimination
- Family status discrimination
- Disability discrimination
- Veteran status discrimination

Civic Rights Act (1964) Title VII

The Civic Right Act of 1964 provides employees the right to employment without regard to race, color, nationality, religion, gender, age, or physical and mental ability.

Age Discrimination Act (1967)

The Age Discrimination Act protects candidates or employees who are above forty years of age from workplace discrimination.

Pregnancy Discrimination Act (1978)

The Pregnancy Discrimination Act aims to protect pregnant women from discrimination because of being pregnant.

Americans with Disabilities Act (1990)

The American with Disabilities Act's objective is to protect the eligibility of people with disabilities for employment. As long as they are capable of the job, they should not be denied because of their disabilities.

Your organization can set up programs to broaden job opportunities for disabled workers, women, and minorities. Be cautious of all these potential discriminations in your place of work, especially as an HR manager or business owner.

Harassment Charges

People are harassed in different ways in the office system. Sometimes, it could be as subtle as sexual suggestive looks and moves to bullying and rape.

For instance, sexual harassment is usually expressed via conduct or language of a sexual nature. These behaviors create a vicious work environment. Besides, victims of harassment are often denied promotions and benefits associated with their work.

The Civil Rights Act of 1991 enables victims of sexual harassment to have jury prosecutions and to be compensated where the employer acted with disregard for the person's rights.

Employees only resort to lawsuits when it seems that their complaints are not attended to and when the harassment interferes with their work. You can make a policy about sexual harassment in your workplace, and this must be included in the employee workbook for all workers and new intakes.

Subsequently, the management of your company should aim to attend to sexual harassment complaints immediately. Those complaints should be investigated thoroughly without bias.

Sensitive Information Charges

The management keeps data gathered during hiring and interviews. This information is expected to be kept confidential by the management. Information such as social security numbers, personal addresses, phone numbers, medical information, spousal information, and so on is considered sensitive.

You must keep employee's information very confidential, not just because it's your duty but to avoid legal issues. Employees do not expect their information to be shared with a third party or individual. Clearly draw the line on what information should be made private. Failure to abide by this level of confidentiality could lead to a lawsuit against your company.

Occupational and Health Safety Charges

The Occupational Safety and Health Act protects employees from work hazards and gives employees health security.

Employees must enjoy working in an environment that feels safe for them. This safety comprises both protection from psychological harassment and physical protection.

Employees are human resources in your company. In this way, they serve as a valuable asset to your organization, which you must guide safely in every way possible. Employees' safety at work, especially for construction companies, should always be considered. For instance, offer the provision of a helmet and steel-toed shoes to your employees while onsite.

Payment Discrepancies Charges

HR managers should not be ignorant about the payment for each employee within the company. This will help you guide against an employee who is underpaid or overpaid. Payment discrepancies can result from gender, racial, or religious discrimination. To correct this anomaly, learn to include equal pay law while preparing the company's policies. The Equal Pay Act seeks to put an end to discrimination of employees' wages or salaries.

Minimum Wages Charges

Employees can file charges because of underpayment. Employers are legally accountable to pay minimum wages to their employees according to government law.

The Fair Labor Standards Act (1938) sets the minimum wages for employers and restricts any form of child labor. It also sets payment for overtime.

Retirement Charges

Retired employees can file charges when their retirement income is denied. A retirement charge can also be filed when an employee is not yet seventy years old, and you forcefully terminate the person's job without prior notice.

The Employee Retirement Income Security Act wants to provide the employees' right to pension after retirement.

Leave Charge

Business owners must give employees leave where the employee is ill (sick leave), has just given birth (maternity leave), etc. You should make sure that your organizations' policies and procedures highlight what employees should do if medical or childbirth leave occurs.

The Family and Medical Leave Act gives the employees the right to be paid health benefits and return to their job where they take medical leave. The condition attached to this is that the business owner must have fifty or more employees and that the employee must have been with the organization for at least a year.

The Act also obligates business owners to provide an unpaid leave of up to three months out of a twelve-month period. This is paid to employees with just given birth to a baby. The leave can be for the following reasons: the birth of a child, adoption of a child, illness of a family member, or employee illness.

Employment Equity Act

Employment Equity Act aims to promote equal rights in the workplace. It gives consideration in employment to women, minorities, persons of color, and people with physical or mental disabilities.

The Immigration Reform and Control Act seeks to make sure that legal immigrants are employed. This also ensures that immigrants with no working permit are not employed.

Employee Rights

Employee rights such as minimum wage, sick days, work hours, vacation time, and severance provisions are established by law and considered employment standards.

The Wagner Act intends to affirm employees' right to join the union of their choice without discrimination. The Act also stops employers from unfair labor practices. So, business owners must adhere to their organizations' policies and procedures.

Bargaining Agreement Charges

If there is union recognition by an organization, and one of the unions is selected to represent the organization's employees, the employer and the union are expected to meet. Both parties will choose a satisfactory time to meet and reasonably bargain about wages, hours, etc. The Wagner Act of 1935 made it legal for most employees to organize or join unions.

Taft – Hartley Act (1947)

The Taft-Hartley Act tasks unions to bargain with employers reasonably. The Act enjoins union representation of all employees covered by labor agreement lawfully and makes sure the union will not deal harshly with employers.

Bargaining agreements between employer and employees can be reneged upon by the negligence of the employer. If a disagreement occurs, specific rules for negotiation, mediation, and arbitration are made. The conflict can cause lawsuits and penalties if all fail to resolve it.

Casualization

Business owners want to cut down on organizational costs, so they underpay employees and cut their working benefits. Many business owners see this as a strategy to reduce costs. This is called Casualization.

Casualization is the use of nonstandard and illegal work arrangements by employers. Employees are underpaid. They do not have the right to medical and other benefits, or the right to join a union. But the legal implications of Casualization are numerous. As an employer, endeavor to avoid the situation of enslaving employees and trampling on their rights.

Undue Termination of Appointment

Employees might feel that their appointment or service contracts were unduly terminated as retaliation for participating in union action, such as strike action, for example.

Undue termination can also be because of discrimination or harassment. As an employer, be careful when terminating the contract of service of an employee. You must try to go through the standard protocols.

Personal Injury

Employers' negligence can make workplace injuries a common occurrence. You need to create a culture of employees' safety in the workplace and try to respond to all safety issues at once. These steps help to prevent personal injury charges.

Overtime

Working overtime is something employers cannot predict and not avoid. All you need to do is monitor the number of hours employees work and make sure that they are paid accordingly.

The U.S. Government has a stipulation for payment of overtime in the workplace. For instance, if an employee in your company works 40 hours per week and earns $10 an hour, the take-home pay would be $400 per week. An additional ten hours of overtime would mean a $15 per hour pay rate for those ten hours of overtime. The overtime pay would amount to $150, so the gross employee pay for that week due to the overtime would be $550.

It could become a legal issue if your employee worked extra-time, above 40 hours, without receiving additional payment for it.

Legal Considerations Tips and Warnings

A small or medium-scale business should not ignore the legal considerations to operate smoothly. Here are a few legal consideration tips and warnings for business owners.

- **Own Up to Errors**

Things might not always go as planned. Let it be known why you cannot meet deadlines or expectations. Own up to the error and be sincere about it. When you try to cover up a mistake in the organization, you are creating even worse problems than the earlier one. This might eventually lead to trust issues and legal problems. So, HR managers or business owners should accept responsibility for their mistakes and make amends where necessary.

- **Take Legal Advice Only from Lawyers**

Different situations require different legal advice. For instance, do not try to imitate another company's problem-solving strategy. It might not fit into yours. Your specific circumstance may require you to seek legal advice first before implementing a strategy.

Always seek advice from your company's attorney to avoid legal crises that could cause irrevocable damages.

- **Be Sure You Know What Your Organization's Policies and Procedures Are**

You must use your employees' handbook as a written document to guide your decisions and choices about employee-related matters. Strive to protect yourself from legal exposure by complying with your employee handbook, company policies, and procedures. By doing these, you are telling your employees you are who you say you are.

- **Create Compliance Action Plans**

Having a compliance action plan guides your organization from the risk of non-compliance to human resources management relevant laws. Compliance Action Plans need not be the same for all businesses. The type of business, number of employees, and the law of business jurisdiction affect the implementation of the compliance Action plan to prevent non-compliance.

- **Anticipate Changes in the Law**

Government law changes occasionally. As the law changes, make sure that your policies and procedures are updated to comply with the current laws affecting human resources management.

Occasionally, the price of adherence might be huge. Understand that it cannot be as high as the cost your organization will incur with lawsuits and penalties.

- **Onboarding Processes**

Be sure that training is done on the organization's policies and procedures during the onboarding process. This will make certain that new employees know their rights and the organization's vision as they started work.

- **Train the Trainers**

Training your managers on relevant laws, their compliance, and their non-compliance implications will help to make sure everyone abides by the organization's policies and procedures.

When managers are well trained, they can easily make sure that employees undergo training on the use of their office equipment and the best work practices. You should not infer that the employees understand what there is to do. You need to train them and do that as often as you can. Enforcing compliance with the working environment regulations will save your organization from legal exposure.

- **Avoid Favoritism**

Your organization's policies and procedures must apply to all employees. Verify that all employees adhere to the same standards. Avoid prioritizing one employee over another, especially in a situation that requires equal disciplinary action.

- **Always Properly Document**

This guarantees the company's safety in times of crisis. Always create proper documentation of all records, such as employee reviews, performance evaluations, attendance records, etc. These will help you to avoid legal issues in the future.

Legal consideration is in the best interest of both the employee and the business. Any business that will thrive must abide by the rule of law and stay true to the company's policies.

Chapter 9: Five Common HRM Mistakes to Avoid

What are you not doing well that seems to affect the company's growth? What still lags in your management skill? What are the common HRM mistakes you must avoid? This chapter is to enlighten new HR professionals, business owners, and existing HR managers on the mistakes you trivialize, which can have severe consequences on the business. This chapter will make you see that though HR managers are the lifelines of the business, and they are vulnerable to making certain mistakes that are detrimental to the company.

Businesses remain strong if their employees work together as a team. You might have a great product, but with bad employees, the business will crash quickly. Most times, the employee issue occurs during recruitment. Sometimes, it can be the inability of an HR manager to place employees together successfully as a team.

Many businesses lose their best workers because of negligence in the hands of the HR manager. Employees are not slaves you control here and there as you wish. They are people who have needs and seek an environment where their contributions are recognized.

You know that the best employees are those who do the job well and are happy because they see themselves as a fundamental part of something important. Lack of relationship between managers or business owners and employees makes you lose your best workers to demonstrate a power struggle.

Most employees feel a sense of recognition when you openly appreciate their contribution to the company. They also appreciate it more when you seek their opinion about matters that pertain to the company's growth. You now understand that recognition and open communication are major factors that increase productivity among employees.

Your employees are the ones in active service. They understand the day-to-day business operation. Your employees understand what works and what does not work, so seeking their opinion before a decision is never a bad idea. What matters is the growth and productivity of the business. But failure to recognize employees' feedback can be detrimental to the business.

You now see that a mistake on the HR manager's part could damage the organization. However, you don't have to continue making these mistakes as an HR manager before you can discover the right way. Many of these mistakes can be avoided. Below are five (5) common mistakes to avoid as an HR manager or small business owner:

1. Lack of Updated Employee Handbook

An employee handbook is a vital document for every business. This document contains the summation of all your company's working policies, vision, mission, work culture, and values. Every employee, either existing or new staff in your company, must have a copy of the company's handbook because it balances the company's operation with the management expectations from employees.

The handbook formalizes the company's policies, which each employee must strictly abide by. Employees do not necessarily have to agree with the policies. Still, you must make sure that they acknowledge the receipt of the handbook with the employee's signature clearly shown.

Many small and medium scale businesses have an employee handbook because of the harmful implications of running a business without it. Your company without an employee handbook makes it easy for any Tom, Dick, and Harry to onboard your team and leave at will. The handbook guides against insubordination among employees and becomes similar to an official document that approves a worker's right standing in the company.

The handbook contains both legal policies and employment ethics for every employee. The challenge is that most HR managers do not review and update their employee handbooks. For instance, when was the last time you updated your employee handbook? Was it two years ago, five years ago, ten years ago, or never? An outdated employee handbook conveys the wrong impression to employees since most of your previous company policies might contradict current work guidelines. This is why you must constantly review yours.

Why You Must Review and Update Employee Handbook

Since the employee handbook contains the company's policies, and work ethics for each employee, review these policies constantly. An outdated handbook is highly unprofessional and does not reflect the company in a good light. This is why I would like to share with you the reasons you need to review your company's handbook periodically.

Note: You must know that the employee handbook is not the general rule for all businesses. It defines the uniqueness of your business. So, you can either review it yourself as an HR manager, or you can consult with the company's attorney.

- It protects the company from lawsuits- In a litigious society, you cannot be too conscientious of the law within your jurisdiction. The government renews employment laws, and these laws must not negate your company policy. To save yourself from court cases regarding your company policies, update it following your company's location or territory's laws. Franklin Wolf, an attorney with Fisher Phillips in Chicago, made it known that dealing with different local and state requirements in the court of law can be very taxing, but it is avoidable when you keep your company policies updated.

- It promotes the organization- The employee handbook is a representation of your company to the employee. It should reflect the company's value for its employees and not just retirement plans that have become obsolete. You must show – within your handbook – that you care for their welfare. This should include revised health care policies, educational plans, insurance, and modern-day benefits in the workplace.

- Employee handbook must intensify on Privacy Laws- The company must enact policies against data breach and public dissemination of private information that relates to the company. For example, a review of social media use and how employees handle customers' information is necessary to avoid a data breach among employees.

2. Lack of Proper Documentation for Employees' Evaluations

How can you establish a performance improvement plan for your employees without proper documentation? Or how can you reward, recognize, and respond to employees' needs without documentation? You must not underestimate your documentation because it is exactly what is needed to evaluate employees' attitudes at work, performance, behavior, and work history.

Lack of proper documentation weakens the HR manager's decisions and his or her ability to make the right choices. Your documentation should contain employees' data, performance analysis, reward and recognition plans, salary structures, promotions, and so on.

As an HR manager, your decision on an employee's performance must not be based on assumptions but on facts collected about the employee over time. Employees' performance management cannot be effective without an accurate record of the employees' attitudes to work, their understanding of the job roles, and their abilities to meet the company's goals.

Many employees do not know what their role entails or who to consult for complaints. They assume a lot about their duties and the organization, so it will become difficult to evaluate such employees if their job role is not well spelled out or the channels of complaints are not known.

Weak Documentation for Performance-Based Evaluation

HR managers must clearly document how much employees perform in the role assigned to them. It then means that weak documentation of an employee's job role will lead to bad performance. You cannot perform well on what you do not understand. This is the case of a poorly written job description for employees. Below is the weak documentation that might cause low performance evaluation:

• Writing hard or soft statements- The HR manager must be professional in writing employees' behavior to work, both laudable actions and the ones that need improvement. You must not sound vague or hastily generalize an employee's attitude to work. For example, it is unprofessional for an HR manager to write this:

Mark is lazy at his job. He does not deliver projects within the time frame given.

Instead, write it this way:

Jan 2: Mark resumes as a new employee in the company.

Jan 9: He completed his onboarding process with his first task. Mark submitted the assignment late.

Jan 21: Mark delayed in presenting the report required of him. He said he needed assistance on how to go about it.

HR manager: What help do you need? What information would be relevant? James and John in the sales department will help Mark make progress on the report.

This does not mean an HR manager should sound soft to the point of losing the value of what you intend to document.

- Incoherent job expectation - You will be confusing yourself and employees when the documented job description differs greatly from the instruction you give to the employee. Most HR managers mistakenly give out job roles to employees but still taking the autonomy of the project. This is called micromanaging and does not help the employee on the job. Give the employee autonomy of the job role.

- No Consequences for Unruly actions - Conflict among workers is unavoidable. But this can be minimized when there are well spelled-out consequences for every action that negates the company's policies. For example, sexual harassment and the smoking of marijuana in the workplace should have specific disciplinary actions. Without these things being documented, employees might take the law into their hands, and that will cause severe problems for the company.

But there are effective documentation practices that help to evaluate employees' performances properly. These are:

- Be clear and succinct - The performance document should be direct and need not sound interesting or friendly. Clearly describe in the document the lapse or incompetence of the employee. Clearly outline company's expectation from the employee.

- Communicate clear expectations - As an HR manager, you must make sure that employees are clear on what the company expects from them. Also, this must be consistent with their job role and description.

- Capture fact in real-time - You do not have to wait until situations get out of hand before you put it under scrutiny. As an HR manager, you must be proactive about employees' disposition to work and take absolute measures without sentiment. Be well detailed when documenting these facts as they serve as reference points during evaluation.

- Performance assessment - Since the job role is clearly defined to the employee, HR managers should periodically make records of the employees' performances on the job. This is both the employees' behavior and job skill.

3. Workplace Favoritism

As an HR manager, you must be careful about how you reward employee's performance so it will not breed resentment in the workplace. To build a formidable workforce, HR managers often create strife rather than teamwork. Unknown to many business owners and HR managers, favoritism, in an attempt to encourage a hardworking employee, actually causes division rather than unity.

What is Workplace Favoritism?

Workplace favoritism is preferential treatment given to an employee for reasons not related to job performance. This is one of the HR manager mistakes that must be corrected. Sometimes, favoritism need not be between the HR manager and certain employees. It could be among a few employees, which will create a tense working environment that does not support teamwork or the company's objective.

Also, workplace favoritism could be in the form of legal issues, like unfair demotion or dismissal of an employee. Sometimes, the HR manager allows their emotions to overtake their sense of judgment, which will leave a rift within the organization. For instance, it is an act of favoritism when you treat an employee unjustly in favor of another. HR managers do not take sides between employees. You are to lead and not to create unnecessary prejudice among employees that could even resort to dismissal.

Below are ways HR managers should avoid favoritism and promote a cordial working relationship among coworkers:

- Communicate mutual expectations- Just as discussed, you rightly have expectations from your workers as an **HR** manager. These expectations must be well communicated so each team member will understand their roles individually.

Equal chances should be given to each worker to empower them to give their best to their assigned tasks. This equality keeps favoritism away from the workplace.

- Appreciate and celebrate little wins quickly- You do not have to wait until the end of the business year before you recognize the selected few's efforts in the company. Your recognition program should be done the moment an employee earned it. Celebrate excellent performance. A survey from Forbes magazine reveals that yearly-based reward programs do not affect the employees positively. Most times, it causes hardworking employees, who were not rewarded, to lose their enthusiasm for work. Yet, this type of reward program forms about 87% of what most businesses do.

- Maintain a proper reward system- There are factors to consider in developing a reward and recognition system for your business. This will help you when going off the business-related performance among employees. Hence, it prevents favoritism. A few of these factors could be attendance (how early or late a worker comes to work), efficiency (how much an employee put into the work), and productivity (the progress and achievement on the job).

Besides, enforcing certain rules on some and being relaxed on others with the same rule produces favoritism in the workplace. Every worker must be treated fairly, and you must not allow sentiment to overrule your judgment. Speak to your employees in the same manner across the board. Do not soften your approach for some and appear too strict for others.

4. Poor Hiring Process and Inadequate Training

How do you source for potential candidates for a vacant position? What questions do you ask during the interview session? What are your plans for onboarding, and what is the growth potential for your new employee? These are critical questions that could warrant serious mistakes if you do not look into them properly.

HR managers are quick to roll out advertisements for a vacant position without considering a target audience. Not all age groups, social classes, skill sets, and experience levels will fit into a vacant position in your company. If you do not know what and who you want, you could ruin the whole recruitment process.

Who is your potential candidate? What skill is expected for the vacant position? How many years of experience are needed? Are you in search of young people just leaving school, postgraduate degree holders, or people with a certain number of years of experience? HR managers who do not ask questions like this will end up with the wrong recruitment strategy.

As the HR manager, try not to do most of the talking during an interview. An interview is to assess the candidate, not to sweet-talk the candidate into accepting your offer. So, HR managers should ask questions that relate to problem-solving skills and communication skills. Either in a telephone interview or a one-on-one interview, HR managers must avoid asking questions that only require one-word answers.

For instance, you can ask your candidate how they complete a specific task within short deadlines. Also, you can ask communication skills related questions like, "How would you describe yourself?" Also, you can say, "Tell us about a difficult task you accomplished together or alone and how you were able to overcome this task." When you ask questions like these, it helps to identify if your candidate is a team player. You cannot be wrong when you ask the right questions.

Then hiring is a phase of the recruitment process. HR managers should prepare for the interview beforehand. A candidate may come prepared to talk during the interview, but then is lazy on the job. So, you must know the candidate's strengths, the disposition to stress, attributes, and enthusiasm to take up the role. Once you have chosen your ideal candidate, then the onboarding should be your next step.

Rushed or improper onboarding has little or no lasting or positive effect on new employees. Often, many HR managers see the process of onboarding as a one-time formality of inducting new employees into the work environment. Don't make the mistake of only discussing what you expect from your employees. HR managers must also see that employees grow through their careers through frequent training and personal development. According to Forbes magazine, highly engaged employees are 38% more likely to have above-average productivity.

5. Ignore Employee's Personal Needs

HR managers must understand that employees are humans and must be treated as such. They are people with needs outside the workplace. Sometimes, these needs affect their motivation to work and can cause less effectiveness on tasks.

Employees' inability to meet their personal needs could hinder their productivity in the business. So, HR managers must find ways to accommodate workers' personal issues and attend to them appropriately. This has a way of motivating your workforce because they have a supervisor who is genuinely interested in their wellbeing and not just the company's profitability.

The truth is if your employee refuses to come to work, you cannot run the business effectively. Taking drastic action without bothering to discover the cause behind the employee's absenteeism should be avoided as an HR manager.

Your employees have a life outside the job. Try to know what they are going through and how the company can be of assistance. This is why your company needs to ensure employees. These insurance policies cover employees' personal needs. Remember, a happy employee means greater productivity. So, please do your best to ensure that your employees stay motivated in their jobs.

The best resort is prevention. You do not have to visit the court of law once your company policies, work ethics, and employment law correlates with the Local and State Laws of your jurisdiction. Your employees are crucial to your business's progress, so you must not treat them as though they are insignificant.

Chapter 10: HRM Technology and Trends

The happiness and satisfaction of employees is a priority to a first-rate company. Employees remain loyal to you and your business when you treat them fairly, look after them, care for them, and pay them well. These actions make them see no reason to quit their job. Interestingly, the New Age gave HR managers software that does their job of human management hassle-free.

The impact of the digital revolution on our daily activity is limitless. It has brought tools that promote efficiency, a seamless mode of data exchange, and solved countless human problems in the workplace. Human resources managers all over the world are now adopting the use of technological tools for accurate decision-making that concern the business and the employees.

The Society of Human Resource Management, in collaboration with Workhuman, observed in 2015 that the major challenges of human capital include employee's talent retention, engagement, competitive compensation, and grooming of future organizational leaders. Thus, the need for technological innovation in the HR department to combat these challenges is ever-present.

The Impact of Technological Innovation in Human Resource Management

Technology has a significant impact on businesses, and you, as an HR manager, can harness these benefits and use them effectively. Therefore, the HR function is no longer a tedious role in the organization, considering you can now carry it out seamlessly in these processes:

- **Recruitment Process**

Recruitment of skillful and competent employees is the most important job of any Human Resources expert. The process gets smarter and faster with the involvement of some technological solutions packages such as Goodhire, HireRight, First Advantage, and so on.

Now, what do these tools do? Let's consider Goodhire. Goodhire is a tool that provides employment background checks and screening solutions for businesses of different scales.

This is a must-have tool for any HR manager. It simplifies the background check and screening process, therefore making the recruitment process faster and trustworthy. HireRight and First Advantage also perform similar functions as Goodhire. The tool to use depends solely on the preference of the HR Manager.

- **Improved Employee Management**

Daily Management of the activities of the employees is another major function of the HR department. This can be very time-consuming, and you might spend hours maintaining information about employees. Here is where time and attendance software, such as PurelyTracking, comes to the rescue. It efficiently manages the entire workforce of the company. It reduces the time spent by HR managers on daily employee affairs. PurelyTracking aims at streamlining employees' records, shift schedules, task management, and payroll.

- Safe Document Management

Human Resources software such as UltiPro, Saba Cloud, Workday Human Capital Management, Ceridian Dayforce, Oracle Cloud HCM, and Cornerstone OnDemand assembles your information in one centrally secured location. This allows easy access to information in the company database at any time you need. This software makes sure your information is secure and accessible in critical times.

Human Resource Management Software

HR software is a specially written program that aims to automate HR processes, transactions, compensation, and payroll. When the HR department's day-to-day tasks increase, so does the need for a sophisticated program to help automate the whole process.

The selection of the right HR software to employ is significant. This is because it helps streamline the hiring, firing, benefits administration, and performance management so that you're able to follow up on your employee's success from the point of recruitment to the point of retirement.

Selection of HR Software

There are key elements you need to consider while choosing your preferred HR software. They are:

- User interface: A user-friendly interface with easy navigation is advised.

- Correlation of tools with your legacy software packages: Tools that tie into your legacy software packages should be preferred. These are software options that have been around a long time and still fulfill business needs.

- Services provided by the vendor: Go for software whose vendors provide the services you'll need if the software fails at any point.

Features of Human Resource Software

Some values and capabilities have to be present in any HR software for maximum performance. Some include:

- Applicant Tracking
- Performance Management
- Scheduling and Shift planning
- Benefits Administration
- Online Learning
- E-Learning Authoring

Applicant Tracking (AT)

This feature is concerned with loss prevention of skillful candidates during recruitment because of a mismanaged recruitment process. The software must be able to manage job postings and recruitments of new employees. The best applicant-tracking tool should be able to track the activities of the employees right from the first moment of interaction until the day of retirement.

Applicant tracking tools selected for use must fit the scale of your organization. It depends majorly on the number of users or jobs available and how well your system integrates with your corporate website. If you hire people regularly, you should purchase tools that link back to your company's career page.

A highly recommended application-tracking (AT) tool is the Bullhorn Staffing and Recruitment System. The BullHorn recruiting system allows you to view and edit a candidate's record. It also allows you to enter data into your AT system immediately after meeting the client so that no information escapes you.

Benefits Administration (BA)

What differentiates a good HR in any organization is how fairly their benefits are being administered to employees and staff. This drives and motivates the employees to give their very best.

Benefits Administration software should be capable of two basic things: making the decisions, choices, and plans easy for the HR manager and making it simple for employees to apply for benefits through an automated application system.

Performance Management

Solutions Performance Management features are often being considered by businesses when deciding the HR management system to adopt. Programmers have created software specially designed to suit the need of this organization. This software may come with features for evaluating employees for benefits and compensation, and skill advancement.

A highly recommended tool for this feature is SAP SuccessFactors, which will do an amazing job tracking and reviewing the company's goals during performance review processes.

Schedule of Shift Planning

Activities of the HR Managers that require managing multiple employee shifts can be overwhelming, hence, why the use of the scheduling and shift-planning feature can be of great help. This feature then becomes a must-have for you as an HR manager. It can directly incorporate scheduling into attendance and payroll.

In small businesses, the scheduling is usually managed by using a grid block on a spreadsheet. But using a dedicated scheduling tool gives your work more flexibility.

Top Human Resource Management Software

Here are top recommendations for HRM software tested and recommended by the MCMag editor's choice.

Gusto

This is best for small businesses and is still relevant to the payroll system. It is proven to have an excellent user experience, is flexible, and has good automation. With Gusto, taxes and deductions are automated and calculated by the software.

Your employees are paid and receive digital pay stubs via email. Each employee also gets login details so they can manage their personal information.

Bamboo HR

This software is best for Human Resources Management for small businesses. It acquires and arranges all information gathered throughout an employee's works cycle. It is easy to set up and navigate, but it is expensive compared to other competitive products.

Namely

Namely welcomes new hires to a team with a simple onboarding process. This platform authorizes you to set company-wide goals and track performance throughout the year. It even allows you to create a custom-fit cycle that fits your business. Namely basically takes care of everything related to payroll and its API allows you to connect every system you use, serving as your core system of records.

Deputy

This software is best for scheduling. The program offers complete scheduling of apps with a drag and drop interface. The software can sync employee's pay rates straight from the paid software such as Gusto, ADP, etc.

Berniportal

This software simplifies tasks such as retirement and setting up stock options. It is easy to navigate and operate, but the organization of its subgroup can be confusing.

SAR SuccessFactors

This is used for small businesses, managing various HR functions, such as employee performance, recruitment, alignment, and learning activities.

Cake HR

This provides attendance, performance, and retirement management worldwide. For instance, if your employees request time off, you have to manage them as an HR manager with a spreadsheet and manually notify each. This can be time-consuming and counterproductive.

What if your employees can do it all on their mobile device or computer? They log in and request time off. Once the request is sent to the manager, the manager can either accept or reject it; a confirmation is then sent to the employee.

HRM Trends of 2020

Here are some HR-related issues you should be looking forward to this year – and likely in years to come.

1. Transparency in Payment

Payment transparency is a significant trend because it's moving from paying for a job title to paying for skills. It is believed that soon, employees will be paid based on their skills and how relevant those skills are to the company. This might be a problem because skills are hard to quantify and compensate. If you consider organizations with a specially designed payroll system, you will notice they survive for a longer time.

Payment is an essential part of a job in your employee's life, but it's losing its significance. Consequently, it's necessary to be transparent and fair about it and make everyone understand the rules that guide the process.

2. Data and Cyber Security

Security and terrorism are the number two most pressing problems facing a company even amidst various technologies. The concern for a possible attack on data becomes significant as the data is moved from the cloud for analysis, but there is believed to be an innovation in that aspect this year.

3. Chatbots

Employers want to be available to their employees 24x7 because they want numerous questions answered in almost real-time. With the decreasing administrative capacity, a chatbot would be useful this year.

4. Quantifying of HR

Quantifying HR measures is difficult to achieve. Still, with the rise of digitalization, it is time to measure a specific process's value and measure the return on the people, business, and strategy.

5. Automation

The automation and robotics sectors possess sophisticated tools that enable the HR department to become more productive and solve specific repeated processes quickly. This trend envisions prediction and increased productivity.

7. Employees Experience

Employees can be very demanding. Employers should change their perspective about their employees and see them as a part of their team and not just replaceable workers. This means the quality of HR service must improve and will affect business digitalization.

Chatbot

When a customer or an employee contacts a company's customer service department, it usually takes a long period to get a response. This is because the agent assigned to attend to them is generally looking for the best customer relationship management software and contact center technology. There is a limit to the information they have access to. This is where the Chabot comes in to play.

The Chabot is simply a bot that has to stimulate a conversation with a person at the other end to assist and solve their problems. Chatbots can be useful in customer service and marketing.

HR Chatbot

Incorporating chatbots in the HR department is a blessing. It saves time and performs HR-related tasks accurately.

HR chatbot is a program specially designed for HR activities. The HR chatbot focuses on activities that require individual or personal attention, such as recruitment, training of employees, and building a better employee relationship.

A perfect HR chatbot is programmed with an artificial intelligence system and machine learning algorithms with aspirations to perform HR based tasks.

The HR chatbot allows you to convert applicants into your applicant tracking system, set them up for interviews, or get them into your talent community, depending on the candidate's skills.

Why should you include chatbot in your recruitment processes?

When a good chatbot is actively in place, you can attend to other HR activities. This saves you time because you are sure that your recruitment process is being properly handled. The benefits of the HR chatbot in the recruitment process are almost limitless. Some of which are also discussed below.

Interview Scheduling

Since chatbots have updated time, calendars, and a database, they schedule interviews perfectly. It provides an automated interview scheduling system for your recruitment process. This saves you time and provides you with perfect scheduling at the same time, even more than a human can.

Automated Scheduling

Chatbots can use the natural language process and provide basic questions that can access and evaluate the job seeker's experience. They stimulate conversation with job seekers about their expectations, experience, skills, and how relevant they are to your organization.

For instance, immediately once a job seeker applies for a job, the HR chatbot interacts with the applicant. It performs a pre-screening by asking candidates questions depending on the position applied for. Where the candidate does not complete the pre-screening process, the chatbot notifies the HR manager and sends follow-up mail. If the candidate passes the process, the chatbot sets up an interview.

Text-Based Recruitment

Chatbot provides a text-based recruitment system where candidates apply for jobs via texting a short code and being screened via text. This method of recruitment is useful in places like billboards and presentations where texting is easiest.

Candidate Experience

Chatbots can act as customer service, acting as standby to answer any question asked by the candidate. From questions on processes and status of the application to the enlightenment of information such as policy, benefits, etc. found in the employee's handbook, a chatbot can answer these and more for potential candidates.

Artificial Intelligence

Most chatbots have an artificial intelligence system and a natural language learning process, which helps them communicate efficiently with candidates.

Return of Investment of HR Chatbot

Measuring the return on investment, your HR chatbot does not require special skills or analysis. The chatbot functions to get more job applicants to your channel. Consequently, you can access its efficiency by the number and quality of new hires coming from the chatbot.

Now, you might be wondering how you track the effectiveness of your chatbot. Here are some metrics to use while tracking an HR chatbot.

- Conversion Rate: This is the number of candidates that apply to your applicant-tracking system via interacting with the chatbots that are newly integrated on your career websites.

- Quality of Applicants: Your chatbot pre-screens candidates by asking them questions that measure their experience and skills before short-listing them for an interview. Thus, a quality list of applicants bares assured.

- Time Saved: With the use of the HR chatbot, you, as an HR manager, can save quality time by performing other HR tasks while chatbots manage your recruitment process. To analyze this, you compare the time the chatbot takes to complete these tasks to that of your team. Then you should be able to track how efficient your chatbot is.

Machine Learning

Another technology currently causing a revolution in streamlining and improving HR function is machine learning.

Machine learning technology leverages artificial intelligence technology. This allows systems to learn and improve from experience automatically without the need to be updated regularly.

Improvement of natural learning has helped to create smart chatbots that can handle HR tasks. Machine learning has also improved significantly by handling many tedious, repetitive, and time-consuming HR tasks.

What are the applications of machine learning to HR? Here are ways machine learning is improving HR.

- Application Tracking: Machine learning applications can track new hires in an automated process, which saves time and work. It promotes fair and unbiased recruitment. The machine learning system uses data collected during the application system to determine if a candidate is suitable for a job or not. Tools such as Hiringsolved and Plum.io can be used for this process.

- Personalization: With various algorithms, the machine learning system is able to understand the unique needs of your employees and provide them with targeted and personalized training and rewards.

- Recruitment of skillful candidates: Companies like LinkedIn make use of machine learning to seek suitable candidates based on artificial intelligence algorithms.

- Improved recruitment accuracy: Machine learning can help HR in the recruitment process by reducing errors and saving time. This also eliminates human bias, and subsequently, only qualified candidates are selected.

Digital human resource strategy is fast becoming the latest trend in the field of human resource management. This is to show that HRM now tilts towards digital development, and any organization that desires to thrive at this time must embrace technological development.

APPENDIX: Human Resources Glossary

C

Career development- Career development refers to programs designed to shape a desired character, talents, and profession with modern-day and future opportunities within the company.

Chatbot- A software that controls automated online responses.

Checkr- Recruitment software used to check the background of your candidates during screening.

Compensation- The approach a business owner adopts by giving monetary value or non-monetary value to their employees.

E

Employee handbook- This document contains the summation of all your company's working policies, vision, mission, work culture, and values.

Employee Relations- The positive relationship between an employer or HR manager and their employees.

G

Goal setting- A technique used by employees or organizations to accomplish tasks.

H

Hawthorn Effect – The principle that a company can improve employee performance by communicating their concern for problems by improving employee work conditions as observed by researcher George E. Mayo.

Hierarchy of Needs – A concept that people will constantly try to meet a sequence of needs such as physical needs (food and shelter) to spiritual needs (self-actualization) as discovered by psychologist Abraham Maslow.

Human Resources Management (or HRM) - is the management of the workforce within an organization by developing policies, strategies, and plans that enable the employees to work towards giving the business a competitive advantage.

J

Job Description – A written document explaining the qualifications and responsibilities of the job being offered, based on the job analysis. This document usually includes an outline of the position, detailed tasks required of the position, and who the employee will report to.

M

Machine Learning – This is a type of artificial intelligence (AI) that allows the computer to learn without human programming. An example of this would be a survey tool assisting Human Resources to document and understand why employees leave their position or stay with the company.

Multitasking- The ability to manage many tasks without becoming out of balance.

O

Onboarding- Frequently used to describe the process involved in bringing new workers into (on board) a new workplace.

P

Payroll- A document that contains the record of a company's employees and staff, which is used to process the paycheck of each employee. This usually includes hours worked, wages or salaries, bonuses and commissions earned, net pay and deductions taken, vacation and sick pay and any contributions made to pension or health insurance plans.

Performance Management- Aims to optimize employee performance by giving a frequent reward system for employees to increase their efficiency and that of the organization.

R

Recruitment Software- A software specially designed for HR managers for the process of recruitment.

Recruitment- Finding the right candidate out of a vast population of job seekers for a vacant position.

S

SWOT- An acronym for strengths, weaknesses, opportunities, and threats.

T

Talent sourcing- Involves identifying, researching, and networking with prospective candidates to discover the individual best fit for the job out of other potential candidates.

Theory X- Stands for the set of traditional beliefs that are negative, fixed, and inflexible.

Theory Y- Is positive, active, and flexible with an emphasis on self-direction and integrating individual needs with organizational demands.

References

15 Key Human Resources Roles | AIHR Digital. (2019, January 29). AIHR Digital.

https://www.digitalhrtech.com/human-resources-roles/

A Guide to Top HR Legal Issues. (n.d.). Www.Hrtechnologist.com.

https://www.hrtechnologist.com/articles/hr-compliance/a-guide-to-top-hr-legal-issues/

All You Need to Know about Employee Relations. (2020, April 14). AIHR Digital.

https://www.digitalhrtech.com/employee-relations/

Bodi, V. (2017, October 7). How Technology Is Changing Human Resource Management. Hppy.

https://gethppy.com/hrtrends/technology-changing-human-resource-management

Glossary of Human Resources (HR) and Employee Benefit Terms. (n.d.). Advos.

https://advos.io/resources/glossary-of-hr-and-benefits-terms/

Human Resource Management - What is HRM? - Definitions - Functions - Objectives - Importance - Evolution of HRM from

Personnel management - What is Human Resource? (Defined) Human Resource

Management Topics - Labor Laws - High Courts & Supreme Court Citation. (2008). Whatishumanresource.com.
http://www.whatishumanresource.com/human-resource-management

ilearnlot - Learn Concept of Business, Economics, Management. (2019). Ilearnlot; ilearnlot. https://www.ilearnlot.com/

Inc, S. S. (2018, April 11). Role of technology in human resource management. YourStory.com.
https://yourstory.com/mystory/70860d77ec-role-of-technology-in

Labor Relations Training From UnionProof. (n.d.). Labor Relations Stories from Union Proof. Retrieved from
https://blog.unionproof.com/

Legal Issues Affecting HR Managers (Know Your HR Law) - Factorial. (2020, April 17). Factorial Blog.
https://factorialhr.com/blog/legal-issues-hr-law/

[MUST READ] Roles & Responsibilities of HR Managers in Growing Organizations. (2019, April 23). SumHR - Employee Attendance, Leaves and Payroll Management Software.
https://www.sumhr.com/hr-manager-role/

Performance Management Strategy - A Quick Guide. (2018, March 6). CIPHR.

https://www.ciphr.com/advice/an-effective-performance-management-strategy/

Pollock, S. (2018, January 7). 6 Strategies for Effective Performance Management - HR Daily Advisor. HR Daily Advisor. https://hrdailyadvisor.blr.com/2018/01/11/6-strategies-effective-performance-management/

SmartRecruiters Team. (2018, June). Recruitment. Smartrecruiters.com;

https://www.smartrecruiters.com/resources/glossary/recruitment/

Stevenson, M. (2019, August 26). 10 Tips for Recruiting the Best Talent. HR Exchange Network. https://www.hrexchangenetwork.com/hr-talent-acquisition/articles/10-tips-for-recruiting-the-best-talent

The Best HR Software for 2020. (n.d.). PCMAG. https://www.pcmag.com/picks/the-best-hr-software

The Difference Between Payroll & Compensation. (n.d.). Small Business - Chron.com. https://smallbusiness.chron.com/difference-between-payroll-compensation-23487.html

The Top 13 Best Recruiting and HR Chatbots - September 2020 | SelectSoftware Reviews. (n.d.). Www.Selectsoftwarereviews.com. Retrieved from https://www.selectsoftwarereviews.com/buyer-guide/hr-chatbots

Top 7 Legal Issues Faced in Human Resources Professionals - WiseStep. (2018, May 16). WiseStep. https://content.wisestep.com/legal-issues-faced-human-resources/

Valamis. (2020). Valamis. https://www.valamis.com/hub/performance-management

What is Onboarding? - Human Resources Degrees. (2016). Human Resources Degrees. https://www.humanresourcesmba.net/faq/what-is-onboarding/

writepass. (2017, February 8). Human Resource Management Approaches. The WritePass Journal. https://writepass.com/journal/2017/02/human-resource-management-approaches/

There are plenty of good resources about—some free and some paid for. These include project management forums and software, as well as books that you can use to acquire a deeper understanding of a particular methodology.

Eric Ries' *The Lean Startup* is a useful guide for startups and smaller businesses. You don't have to know anything about Agile to get started with this book. It talks about Lean methodology, and it is highly business-orientated, unlike some books which get stuck more into the nuts and bolts of project management processes.

Coaching Agile Teams by Lyssa Adkins is a good book if you are struggling with introducing Agile to a more traditional management environment. It talks about how to create the right corporate culture for Agile teams and empower your project team members.

Mitch Lacey's *The Scrum Field Guide: Practical Advice for Your First Year* reviews basic practices and helps you get started managing Scrum meetings and sprint sessions. It is well rooted in real-world situations and includes information on managing contracts, which you will need if you have an external customer at the end of your project or process. Lacey warns, though, that although Scrum is very adaptable, you shouldn't cherry-pick your favorite bits—you have to commit yourself to Scrum in its entirety to get the best out of it.

Kenneth S Rubin's *Essential Scrum* is a key text for Scrum Masters, focusing on how the Scrum roles fit together and how sprints work. It is perhaps a little less user-friendly for the beginner than Lacey's book, but if you want to live the Scrum Master life, it ought to be on your bookshelf.

In the world of Lean Six Sigma, you could get *Lean Six Sigma for Dummies*—it is great for an entry point, though by the time you are thinking about black belt certification, you will probably have left it behind. It is very focused on Lean Six Sigma—you won't learn about other project management methodologies, but you'll be really well informed on Six Sigma by the time you're finished. A soberer approach to the subject, but equally good at explaining Six Sigma basics, is Greg Blue's *Six Sigma for Managers*. Greg is a Master Black Belt and a well-respected consultant, and the book is a clear and well-written explanation of what Six Sigma is and how it works.

For value stream mapping, the "Bible" is Karen Martin and Mike Osterling's *Value Stream Mapping: How to Visualize Work and Align Leadership for Organizational Transformation*. That is a long title, but the book itself is a very practical guide to the subject. If you are going to be doing extensive work in this area, it's really useful. Or you could consider John Shook and Mike Rother's

Learning to See: Value Stream Mapping to Add Value and Eliminate Muda, which you can use as a workbook. However, it has a heavy focus on manufacturing—if you are in services, it may not be as useful.

Lean Analytics: Use data to Build a Better Startup Faster takes you through the subject in real detail. If you are lost in a fog of data and can't see which KPIs you need to look at right now, this book will help you. If you don't understand how some of the KPIs relate to your business strategy and priorities, it will help you with that, too. Anyone who lives in the land of click-throughs and conversions needs this book.

Robert Maurer's *One Small Step Can Change Your Life: The Kaizen Way* is a great resource for getting started with Kaizen. It is an inspirational guide to how you can bring Kaizen to your daily life. The same author's *The Spirit of Kaizen: Creating Lasting Excellence One Small Step at a Time* is also an introductory text but focuses on how to get Kaizen working in your organization. It is full of practical tips, real-world stories, and tools that are ready to use.

On the other hand, if you are ready to get into Kaizen in-depth, Shigeo Shingo's *Kaizen and the Art of Creative Thinking: The Scientific Thinking Mechanism* is your go-to tome. Shingo worked with Toyota and other major Japanese companies to improve their production processes, and the book is jam-packed full of useful stuff. If there is a key takeout, it's that you have to learn how to think outside the box—but that you can start to do so in quite a methodical way! It is a heavyweight book, but managers who have used it absolutely rave about it—it's the kind of book that you will go back to again and again.

If you work in software and want to implement kanban, you will love Arne Roock's *Stop Starting, Start Finishing*. It is an enjoyable, humorous read, but it is great for teams and managers that are new to kanban and focuses on how you can use kanban to limit work in progress and get more tasks actually done. You can also download a free ebook, the *Kanban Roadmap: How to Get Started in Five Easy Steps* from https://info.planview.com/kanban-roadmap-_ebook_lad_en_reg.html. Give a copy to every member of your team, and you have made a great start on the kanban journey.

Trello (trello.com) is a great software choice for managing kanban boards. It is a really simple app, but you can refine your kanban board by adding comments, attachments, or due dates to the cards. It's collaborative, so you can use it to link all your project members, whether within or outside your organization. And it runs on all kinds of Android and Apple devices so that you can easily keep a distributed project team in sync.

KaiNexus Software (kainexus.com) is also worth a look if you are headed the full Kaizen route. It has a fascinating and frequently updated blog, too, with reports from conferences, articles about new approaches, or about companies that are implementing Kaizen and Kaizen culture in general.

Projectmanagement.com is the Project Management Institute's web page, and it is one of the best places to see what's going on in project management, whatever particular flavor of **PM** you have adopted. There are plenty of articles covering a diverse range of subjects, from ethics to real-world case studies, specialized tools, and best practice tips for particular industries or tasks. PMTips.net is another great site with tons of listicles (like "5 ways to improve product testing"), career advice, how-to's ("Rescue and recovery of projects", which everyone will need someday!), and tips.

Manufactured by Amazon.ca
Acheson, AB